# On the Benefits of Friendship

Isabelle
Graw

# On the Benefits of Friendship

TRANSLATED BY BEN CATON

Sternberg Press

To my friends

The following is based on experience and fantasy alike. Adapted from personal encounters, the situations I describe have been condensed and re-formed in a literary mold, and each figure is a stylized composite of real-life acquaintances. Social-theoretical considerations also flow into these individual accounts of friendship, revealing them to be both unique and indicative of certain social structures. My observation that friendships are neither entirely free of self-interest nor dictated by it is demonstrated through my relation to the peculiar cosmos of the art world. And by drawing upon the literary genre of the fictionalized diary—exemplified in writings by Marie Luise Kaschnitz or Max Frisch—I aim to include elements of social criticism. It is my intention throughout to raise both a lament to the pitfalls of "useful" friendships and a hymn to true friendship.

"If you ask me who here speaks, which I,
then it is my own and yet again not;
from whom would only the own I ever
speak."

Marie Luise Kaschnitz

**7.27.2020**

My longing for friendship was particularly pronounced on waking up this morning. This may have been due to my cloudy mood. I reached for my phone to banish the feeling of gloom with a short conversation with my friend Solange. The fact alone that she granted me her full attention during this exchange gave me courage for the day. I took strength from the fact that she is someone to whom I can always turn, whatever my state. Especially in those moments when everything appears futile and I lack the vigor to face the day, I need her friendship like the air I breathe.

My need for social bonds was always very strong, possibly as a result of coming from a largely dysfunctional family. In order to escape it, I have sought ersatz families among my friends since childhood. I hoped these "families" would show an interest in me as a person, as my parents were incapable of doing (at least in any real measure); they were too occupied with themselves, and it never occurred to them to consider their children's feelings. Children at that time—it was the 1960s and 1970s—were supposed to behave. My siblings and I were expected to resign ourselves to a situation where our father was permanently absent and our mother despaired at being constantly cheated on with younger women. Left alone with three children, she was understandingly overwhelmed. When, after several attempts, she finally succeeded in separating from him, she stumbled into no-less-unhappy love affairs that often left her physically incapacitated. In my memory, my mother spent a large part of her time in bed during this period, plagued by gallbladder pains. The fact that she hid the divorce from us for several months caused me to turn away from her in disappointment in my teenage years; the bond of trust between us had been too profoundly shaken.

I turned my attention elsewhere, seeking alternatives in the families of my friends. I spent a lot of time with a relatively intact family who were our neighbors, regularly spending the night at their house. Strict Catholics with many children, they even took me along on family vacations; the group photos taken on these trips bear witness to my efforts to belong, despite me visibly not belonging. I rarely spent much time at home, and when I did, I immediately retreated to my room and my readings (from Christine Nöstlinger's *Fly Away Home* to, eventually, Dostoyevsky's *Crime and Punishment*). When I wasn't reading, I escaped into daydreams in which I imagined a future life where I would be supported by like-minded friends. I envisioned a sympathetic social environment that would encourage, welcome, and truly understand me. The sense of unhappiness I associated with my family was commensurate with the hopes I placed on friendship groups and scenes of my own choosing.

My first experiences of a chosen friendship group were with the *Elbvorortsclique*, a group of privileged children of bourgeois Hamburg families, which met up in tennis and hockey clubs or on Waitzstraße, a shopping street in Hamburg-Othmarschen. This clique was symptomatic of the social seclusion of such milieus at the time: it only consisted of white people. Its homogeneity in terms of race and class wasn't apparent to me at the time. And I only realize now how little tolerance there was for difference. This scene was no idyll in other respects as well: it was hierarchical, and members who were seen as not really belonging were marginalized and shut out. While the threat of exclusion hung over my head like the sword of Damocles, my membership in the clique nonetheless taught me some of the benefits of life in a community. I imagined myself to be more connected through my relationship to the others, but I also felt stronger as part of a group. The fact that they had accepted me seemed to distinguish me and elevate my status. And yet my personal circumstances (divorced parents, small townhouse instead of spacious villa) meant I occupied an ambivalent position within the group: as the child of a less wealthy (but still privileged) family, I found myself somewhat on the margins, while my unconventional family situation made me more "interesting." For the first time, I experienced my status as a "child of divorce" as a distinguishing characteristic rather than just a social stigma.

And yet my parents' separation also produced a sort of psychological split within me. I was filled with longing for a well-off but absent father and had to cope with cramped conditions in my everyday life, sharing a small townhouse with my mother and siblings. Internally, I was torn between rage at my father who had left us, but who also stood for an aspirational life of luxury, and the pain I felt at seeing the more modest conditions of my mother, who offered me a greater degree of emotional security. It was therefore fitting that I seemed to stand with one foot in the clique and one foot outside it—a feeling of not belonging that would continue to accompany me later in life. This sense of alienation was uncomfortable, and nothing would have made me happier than switching places with a friend from an intact household. My imposed distance also forced me to take a removed perspective, leading me to record quasi-sociological observations in my diary. Since there was no one in the group with whom I wanted to share these considerations, I began an inner dialogue regarding my social life, which continues to this day. While I would have happily foregone this outsider perspective as a teenager, it's possible I benefited from it in the long run.

The input of certain male experts within the group meant that we were relatively well informed about music; in my memory, we constantly listened to Earth, Wind & Fire. There was also much discussion of politics, with controversial statements by clique members often mirroring the conservative or left-liberal attitudes of their parents. With a few exceptions, barely anyone read. The numerous books I devoured from my mother's well-stocked library I discussed with my younger brother, who read a lot himself.

The clique was the place where my fashion sense was first honed—the standard outfit was a V-neck sweater, ideally cashmere, combined with expensive La Scarpa suede boots. I was determined to acquire this costly uniform since it promised a feeling of security and a more confident demeanor. Luckily, my father was willing to buy me the expensive fashion items I coveted. In doing so, he paid off his emotional debt to me in installments. His new house did not include a children's room, as if there was no room for me and my siblings in his life; instead, he demonstrated his affection by giving us money and occasionally clothing us. And yet these gifts were unable to alleviate the pain I felt at not being allowed a place in his life.

Back to my youth in the *Elbvorortsclique*. It was in this social framework that I was first confronted with the fleetingness and fragility of friendship. One day, my best friend at that time, a clique member herself, ended things with me without any fanfare. The reason she so abruptly turned away from me—as I would learn years later from others—was her frustration at my behavior during a vacation in Biarritz. My enthusiasm for the flirting culture in France had led me to go out instead of caring for my friend, who lay in bed ill with gastroenteritis. Unfortunately, she never communicated her understandable anger and disappointment to me; we lacked both the courage and the language for a heart-to-heart discussion about our friendship. Irritations and injuries were only vaguely perceived within the group; they were simply filed away, never really entering our consciousness. To talk about what had happened was unthinkable. Instead, my friend immediately teamed up with a far more popular girl from the clique. I can still see them zooming off together on their chic Vespas, leaving me behind on my bicycle.

Other members of the clique later let me know that I was guilty of gross misconduct during the vacation, and so it was only right that my friend turned away from me. All of this I gathered in passing, since no one spoke to me about it openly. But from the change in their behavior toward me, and through vague insinuations, I was able to infer that my friend had broken with me and reoriented herself. I lost her to another without words or conflict, which greatly upset me, and yet I could not admit to this feeling, let alone verbalize it. That I've never again had one single best friend is possibly connected to this early experience of loss in my teenage years.

I now have a network of several friends, most of them women, meaning any potential loss of one friend could theoretically be made up for by the others. My friends are not mutually interchangeable, however; they are singular figures who cannot simply be exchanged for one another. As soon as conflicts or disagreements emerge, I fight to preserve the friendship, mostly through conversations that I hope will clarify things between us. If a conflict does result in deeper injury or rejection, I can be as distraught as a spurned lover. Except that now, no longer bound to a single best friend, I will not be left alone, as I was in my teenage years, should our parting prove unavoidable. There are now several people to whom I can turn in such a situation. In endless conversations, they help me illuminate and analyze the reasons for the friendship's collapse.

**7.30.2020**

That I ended up living in Cologne in the late 1980s was due to the hopes I connected with its art scene and the friendships I might make within it. Even more than with the *Elbvorortsclique*, the art community there followed the model of the chosen family: mostly headed by men, it consisted of more highly regarded or less valued family members and "poorer" relatives who were distanced and marginalized. Here, too, the approach was at once intimately familial and ruthlessly hierarchical. Any woman seeking to assert herself and gain recognition within this male-dominated milieu first had to endure a certain amount of insult and humiliation. In my memory, there were rarely male colleagues who encouraged me or supported me in my endeavors. Instead, they generally attempted to educate me in a manner that is now rightfully scorned as "mansplaining." Or else they subtly let me know that my work didn't really count—by never saying a single word about the texts I published, for example.

The dogged struggle for recognition was familiar to me, since I had already spent years trying to win more respect for myself (and my work) from my misogynistic father. As a young woman, I wanted to be seen and taken seriously by him at any cost; that is, by a man who refused to take women seriously. It was likely for this reason that I felt so at home in the Cologne art world. I even took pleasure in the battle to be seen and heard, as it had long become second nature to me to fight for myself. Business as usual. Only gradually did I realize that the benevolence and support my parents did actually show me in good moments could not always be expected of the members of such a chosen family. In retrospect, the Cologne art-world family far exceeded my family of origin in terms of dysfunctionality. Division, betrayal, and intrigue were all part of the daily agenda; the traditional model of artistic avant-gardes was thus replicated within our network of friends.

As for most of the friendships I entered into with certain Cologne artists, writers, and gallerists during this time, these probably fell under the category of instrumental friendships, which are endemic within the field of art. Friends are valued less for what they are or purport to be and more for the benefits they might offer regarding one's own career. Within the art world—as with other creative fields—a form of friendship dominates that one could describe through the eyes of Aristotle in terms of their utility: friendships with a strong instrumental streak. These, he argues, should not be confused with true friendship, in which the other person is valued for who they are. But as apposite as his description of utility-oriented friendships may be, it overlooks something fundamental: that the borders between true, unselfish friendship and useful friendship are often fluid, at least in my own experience. It's possible to value someone while at the same time wanting something from them. Moreover, in addition to considerations of usefulness, it can sometimes be deeply held feelings that bind one to friends; rational calculation and irrational attraction are tightly interwoven within friendships.

In contrast to Aristotle's reductivist view, the useful friendship should be characterized by the mutual intertwining of self-interest and deep sympathy for the other. While Aristotle's account of the utility friendship is excoriating, I believe this form of friendship can go hand in hand with true feelings and would not condemn it outright. Instead, and partly in view of its current prevalence, my aim is to closely examine and better understand it, especially since I myself cultivated (and even actively sought) friendships during my time in Cologne that were both useful and based on genuine affinities. It was only in retrospect that I realized I primarily sought the friendship of those people who I assumed could benefit me and my work. I did also feel drawn to them because of their charm, wit, amiability, or intelligence, but the position these people held in the art world was—as I see it today—of equal importance to my interest in them. At the same time, this position was usually justified by the fact that they had something interesting to offer or say.

Before the reader of these lines condemns me for my calculating spirit, I would like to add that my friendships in Cologne were generally based on a strong foundation, which might be described as a shared value horizon. Put another way, what connected me to these friends was our common understanding of ourselves as comrades-in-arms, united in our fight for certain theoretical, aesthetic, or political convictions that were anything but mainstream at the time. The instrumental streak within our friendships was therefore rooted in our belief in their objective necessity; it was precisely because we shared a worldview that we connected and became friends.

That I experienced these friendships as decidedly invigorating and motivating was above all due to the fact that they were based on common goals, such as the implementation of certain shared convictions or the (related) mutual advancement of our careers. But the unwritten rule of these relationships was that one's own feelings could under no account be thematized during a meeting or encounter; even the ritual nicety of asking how someone is drew scorn. This resistance to the personal was opportune for me, since I had barely any access to my own feelings as a young woman. To address them in the framework of these friendships would also have struck me as inappropriate, since openly professing one's emotions was decried as hippieish within the subcultures I frequented in the 1980s (punk, new wave). To articulate your feelings was fundamentally off-limits (only later did I realize that this also went hand in hand with a phobic resistance to everything imagined to be "feminine"). For me, what counted above all was the shared fight for a common cause, for which I was only too happy to endure the hard social climate. This quasi censorship of the emotional and interpersonal meant I was free to devote my energies to substantive matters, which suited me perfectly. I found the intensive discussions with my Cologne friends—whether about exhibitions or our feuilleton readings—to be enormously productive, and I would return to my desk inspired and motivated afterward. For it was in exchanges with them that my ideas and plans first matured; ideas and plans that I now began to resolutely put into practice (or, more accurately, into texts).

With his characteristic pathos, Hölderlin once commented that no thought can emerge without first being exchanged in a conversation or a letter to a friend. His observation is exaggerated in its absoluteness, of course, especially since it is entirely possible to develop thoughts without friends—as when conducting a dialogue with oneself, for example. And yet this assertion does have some truth to it with regard to my years in Cologne: without the numerous suggestions and comments made by my friends at that time, my writing practice would surely have been different.

**8.8.2020**

Since many of the friendships I had in Cologne were ultimately somewhat instrumental—and this without me yet being aware of it—their ending was also foreseeable. Aristotle himself noted that the utility friendship can easily be broken; its usefulness eventually runs out, and so it cannot endure. When a person ceases to be useful to us, he claimed, there is no longer any reason to maintain a friendship that was primarily oriented around utility.

Except that—as I have already stated—this utility cannot be so sharply differentiated from emotional factors such as affinity and attraction. Admittedly, I myself have at times left friends behind when their work fell into disrepute and suddenly seemed less relevant, and so of little use to me. At the same time, there were always friends whom I stuck by in times when their work became unpopular, or when they were experiencing great difficulties—simply because I liked them. While my diminished interest in others may in some cases have been motivated by objective considerations, their reduced status made it easier to turn away from them.

However, the reverse situation—of being dropped by friends after becoming unpopular myself—is equally familiar to me. Several years ago, a few of my friends (some of them artists) distanced themselves from me when one of my texts came under fire and I needed their support. Drawing upon the early modern literary technique of the "dialogue with a friend," I had attempted to connect social-critical reflections with the personal in the text. From the frosty or entirely absent reactions of certain friends, I could tell that something was wrong; there seemed to be a broad consensus that it had been unsuccessful. While their objections to my writing experiment may have been entirely justified, they also found ways of indicating that the wind had turned against me. Through offhand and dismissive comments, they indirectly let me know that I had failed, and that I had now catapulted myself out of the arena of serious critics.

My relationship to artists represents a particular field of tension here. Friendships between critics and artists are generally characterized by power and dependency as much as by mutual affinity and support. To be friends with artists is an advantage to an art critic (like myself), since it brings us closer to the "action"; we are afforded an exclusive insight into artistic production, from which our own critical approach can then benefit. And yet to be friends with artists as a critic also causes person and product to become conflated. Should an artist make a positive impression on you as a person, the chances are you will also approve of their work. Objections to their practice are unlikely, since this might endanger both the friendship and your image of them as a person. In fact, I have always insisted that one can raise (constructive) objections to the works of artist friends, and that one must be able to point out their shortcomings without fear of causing offense. This is hard to realize in practice, however, since any extremely critical text inevitably causes resentments of the sort one usually avoids at all costs. It's for this reason that every critic I know shies away from massively criticizing the work of artists they are close to.

There are some artist friends of mine whose work I have supported since the beginning of their careers, for which I was often rewarded with commissions for catalogue texts or talks. In certain cases, these friendships were subsequently characterized by a sort of psychodynamic law: where an artist experienced institutional success that I myself had also contributed to (or at least played some part in), only rarely was I acknowledged. I found it telling that their interest in me diminished at the exact moment the institutional recognition and market success they long desired was finally bestowed upon them. Possibly I reminded them too strongly of a phase in their life when things were not going so well and they were more reliant on me, a dependency they now wanted to shed. Correspondingly, I also sought to free myself from a strong orientation toward their practice in my own work.

While a few of these artists subsequently rose to a higher economic sphere, people like me, who originally helped pave the way for their success, remained at a lower level of the hierarchy. In financial terms, critics in any case occupy the role of the "poor relative," since the fees they command are extremely low when compared to the incomes of the commercially successful artists whose works they occasionally write about. While they can in theory continue to influence the careers of the artists in question, in reality it's rare for critics to distance themselves from artist friends they formerly supported, since this would run the risk of devaluing their earlier engagement with them and damaging their own credibility, which is not in their interest.

That being said, there are also artists who remain loyal to those critics and supporters who assisted them in their early careers. In exceptional cases—especially within the commercial art scene—a further phenomenon can be observed: that of successful artists gifting "their" critics a piece of art in return for their services, thus directly involving them in its potential for future returns. Should its value rise within the auction sphere, the critic will one day be able to sell it in order to, for instance, use the proceeds to buy an apartment. Scenarios such as this, which speak of a compensatory sense of fairness, can be found time and again throughout the history of the art market.

**8.10.2020**

Of the culture of friendship that existed within the Cologne art world of the 1980s and 1990s, it should be noted that it naturally made a difference whether one identified as a man or a woman, or as straight or gay. The experiences of friendship I have gathered here from my own memories are those of a heterosexual cis woman who saw herself as tasked with an intellectual "mission" through which she sought to assert herself within her field. That the path to attention and social recognition is directly dependent on one's friendships is something I must have realized intuitively. But rather than consciously and strategically aiming at such relationships, they seemed instead to fall into place organically. The now-common notion of the network imperative, according to which each personal contact represents an important economic resource, was not yet prevalent at that time, and it simply wouldn't have occurred to me that some of my Cologne friends would one day become legendary artists or important players in the art world. Instead, we saw ourselves as a sort of underground, and the idea that our practices would eventually be rewarded with institutional recognition or commercial success was never taken as a given. It's possible that this lack of conscious calculation was the precondition for the success many from this milieu went on to enjoy in their later careers.

Upon arriving in Cologne in the late 1980s, I met Andreas, an artist who took me under his wing and introduced me to the local art scene. He would take me around to the relevant bars and restaurants in order to introduce me to significant (and mostly male) figures from the scene. My communication with them often had a flirtatious undertone; they seemed to be checking me out and assessing me as a potential romantic partner.

I had instinctively resolved to stop drinking after arriving in the city—most likely as a way of making myself unapproachable. While just a short time before I had spent nights happily drinking gin and tonics in Paris nightclubs, there were no longer any excesses to be enjoyed in my company; my abstinence placed me at a distance and ensured I remained somewhat outside of things. That I decided not to drink alcohol appears in retrospect like a survival strategy; as a woman, I faced a difficult situation within this male-dominated milieu, forced to fight for a position that was never intended for me. To have joined in with their drinking—at least so I feared—could have been my downfall. I didn't want to lose control, which in my mind would have meant handing myself over to the men around me. It was far more important that I remember (and write down) what happened the night before when I woke up in the morning. My boyfriend at the time, Carl, was rarely in Cologne and spent periods living in Paris, which also contributed to my image as a spoken-for (and therefore somewhat unapproachable) young woman whose abstinent lifestyle kept her at a distance. That the Cologne art world nonetheless welcomed me with open arms—even if, as a woman, I was an exception in a male-dominated milieu—seemed to be a stroke of luck at the time.

Within just a few weeks, it was as if I belonged to the social circle of interesting artists and theorists I had always dreamed of. At the same time, I knew that attractive young women were welcomed within this scene, in part so the men could adorn themselves with them. With my short hair, I based my look on Jean Seberg, spending all my money on black suits by then-fashionable labels like Yohji Yamamoto or Comme des Garçons. By my late twenties, I still resembled a teenager who had yet to lose her baby fat (at least in my imagination), which I sought to change through nightly visits to smoke-filled bars and a strict diet (only soup in the evenings). But the androgynous body I longed for, along with sharper facial features and rings under my eyes, refused to materialize.

My youthful appearance and enthusiasm for fashion were simultaneously a curse and a potential advantage. The older men, especially, tended not to take me seriously; one curator even suggested I try my hand in the fashion world, where he thought I would fit in much better. At the same time, I was seen as an "it girl" due to my appearance and demeanor, as a friend from those times recently told me—that is, as someone with a certain media presence and degree of recognition. But

I certainly didn't perceive myself as such at the time. On the contrary, I felt as if I were on the periphery and lacked visibility. It girls can be found in all artistic scenes, not least since they are afforded an important function within them, as bodies for the projection and resonance of others' ideas. Their presence is valued mostly for aesthetic reasons, since they act as a sort of mirror that reflects favorably on the scene, bolstering its self-image. And yet they also help lend it a greater sense of charisma, thus acting as a sort of amplifier for its artistic concerns.

Should an it girl seek to make any claim to having ideas of her own, however (or, as in my case, be unwilling to offer their unconditional support to the dominant belief system within the art world), things can get complicated. In time, I realized that I was essentially forbidden from participating in the "creative flow" of most of the male artists and theorists—exactly as Simone de Beauvoir describes in *The Ethics of Ambiguity*. They allocated me the role of sounding board for their ideas, excluding me from ever making it to their level; according to Beauvoir, admittance to this "level" is the precondition for "new conquests." By refusing me an equal place among them, they cut me off from my future (as Beauvoir formulates it) and turned me into a "thing"—a thing that had been granted a particular function (that of an art critic), but which was fundamentally denied equal status as a creative subject. My position as an art critic fed into this dynamic, since in the eyes of many artists, the primary job of critics was to communicate the concerns of those who actually produced art. In fact, there was a great interest in my own work, which manifested itself in frequent requests for catalogue texts and talks, while beyond this, numerous artists, gallerists, and collectors supported my plans to start my own journal. But despite their considerable support, I had been allocated a place within this milieu that was not seen as genuinely equal by most of its male actors. While some of them were rewarded with respect for their work from the beginning, I had to constantly prove myself anew.

**8.12.2020**

As already intimated, my friendly relationships with the heterosexual male artists of the Cologne art scene were not free of sexual desire. It didn't bother me when they sometimes made their feelings clear, as long as my boundaries were maintained; on the contrary, I enjoyed the feeling of being "wanted" in this way. And naturally, I in turn sometimes projected my own sexual fantasies onto them, including my vision of a relationship that was both romantic and professionally fulfilling. I did however seek to protect myself from the brashest and most macho of them, who might have been dangerous. I refrained from entering sexual or romantic relationships with such artists as a matter of principle, since I imagined they would treat me badly or one day leave me for a younger and more amiable partner. They, for their part, showed no serious interest in me—possibly since I was largely unsuited to the subordinate role of "supportive girlfriend."

Only once did someone's interest in me tip over into a sexual violation. I had set up an interview with an artist. He arrived for our conversation already drunk, while I stuck to my cup of tea. I had studied all his catalogues in preparation, immersing myself in his work; my aim, rather than showering him with praise, was to conduct a heated discussion about the various aspects of his artistic practice. I can barely recall the substance of our conversation today. I only know that the sound quality of the (now lost) recording of the interview was very poor since our voices were drowned out by the sound of him continually refilling his wine glass.

Our meeting had been scheduled for the late afternoon but dragged into the late evening. At some point, he asked me to see him to his room, as he lived in the hotel whose café we were in. His pleading became louder and more urgent: he said he couldn't fall asleep alone; I only had to accompany him, there was nothing more he wanted from me. I initially refused the suggestion, but his vehemence eventually caused me to give in, like a frazzled babysitter who eventually gives the crying child a lollipop to calm them. Seen from today's perspective of the #MeToo era, my decision to follow him to his room was of course hopelessly naive. I was convinced that he had no sexual intentions and that he just wanted me to give him some company—like a distressed child who can't fall asleep alone.

As soon as we entered the room, he locked the door and hid the key. I can't remember how I managed to convince him to open the door again and let me go, but somehow I did. In my fuzzy recollection, I spoke to him softly and reassuringly despite my fear, until he eventually gave up and let me leave. My only precise memory is of the moment he suddenly whipped the key out of the door and hid it. In that terrible instant, I knew I had fallen into a trap.

I spoke to no one about the incident; I wouldn't even have known whom to turn to with such a story. The concept of sexual harassment was not commonplace back then, and so I chalked up what I experienced to an "occupational hazard." To enter friendships with male artists was dangerous for me, not least since the codes were not explicit. A friendly request for assistance could conceal sexual intentions, and good friends could turn out to be aspirant lovers.

**8.18.2020**

There also are happier stories to be reported in this context. Several of my love affairs produced intimate and trusting friendships, and I've remained good friends with most of my exes to this day. One of them—a writer—I would even call a very good friend. He knows my most private fears and weaknesses, and he remains loyal to me even when he believes I'm making a mistake. The reverse is also true: I'm always there for him. I help him during crises in his work or love life, and I stand by him in those rare moments when his popularity seems on the wane. We know each other well, and our loyalty toward one another endures periods of crisis.

Our relationship was always characterized by a strong bond of friendship, whereas it was difficult romantically. The fact that we were once a couple might also make it easier for us to be our true selves with one another—in part, at least. We each cry freely over life's injustices in the other's company. But while we have supported each other for as long as we can remember, this support includes an instrumental element: as an author who holds his books in high regard, I am happy to promote them, while he in turn enriches my texts with his productive comments. We also critique one another, of course; we play the role of devil's advocate, confronting each other with the potential objections of our detractors without ever fully agreeing with them.

But to what extent does the intensity of our friendship—and of my relationship to some of my ex-boyfriends more generally—stem from the fact that we were once lovers? Perhaps the physical intimacy we experienced earlier means our friendship can now be more emotional, closer, less guarded. Beyond this, I am connected to many of my exes by a sort of shared sensibility, and by similar values and political convictions. That these connections were not lost when the relationships ended brings me great joy.

**8.19.2020**

In her book *On Humanity in Dark Times*, Hannah Arendt writes that it is only in misfortune that true friendship proves itself. This is also my experience: during periods where I was plagued by adversity (such as the sudden deaths of my parents), I was supported by just a few from within my circle, who thus revealed themselves to be my true friends. It is only natural that friendships whose focus is primarily on their usefulness should prove to be less resilient; weakened by separation or grief, one simply has less to offer in the eyes of those whose main interest is in reaping the benefits of the relationship.

Even small missteps can cause a thinning in the ranks of one's supporters, as I recently experienced after delivering a contentious talk. During the subsequent dinner, some of my friends and colleagues noticeably distanced themselves from me. I needed their support, but it never came. In my slightly paranoid post-talk mental state, I imagined they had long ago joined the chorus of my fiercest critics but kept it hidden from me until now. For rather than voicing their undoubtedly justified objections about my talk to me directly, they adopted the perspective of those who were determined to use the occasion to discredit me. I couldn't help but sense a certain degree of schadenfreude on the part of these friends and peers—it seemed as if they were secretly happy at the damage to my academic reputation. While this perception might be paranoid, I have often sensed this type of hostility among my fiercest critics and opponents—a barely suppressed feeling that I should just give it a rest, shut up, and disappear.

It should be noted that "useful" friendships of this type rarely survive dark times, such as situations of personal crisis. Anyone whose personal connection to another is based primarily on perceived usefulness will, in all probability, turn away the moment there is no more benefit to be gained from the friendship. In situations where there has been damage to my reputation, some of my friends found subtle, often barely perceptible ways of letting me know I was a persona non grata who had left the zone of relevance—as if I had dropped out of the running of serious contenders. From their increasingly infrequent calls and social invitations, it was clear that they saw less potential benefit from their contact with me under these conditions. All of a sudden, they were too busy to meet in person. Or perhaps I had just become less likeable to them. It's impossible to say to what degree their diminishing interest was due to a loss of professional standing on my part or of sympathy on theirs; most likely it was a mixture of both. As their goodwill faded, they also began viewing my work more critically. Yet it seemed as if their comments echoed the voices of those who had long ago resolved to find my position problematic. My drop in status was further signaled by a tendency to ignore my talks, texts, and books, whose presence was simply no longer acknowledged; it was as if my cultural production could be silenced out of existence.

I remember the numerous meetings with Peter, one of my most long-standing friends in the art world, when I waited in vain for him to comment on something I had published. Peter is an artist who—unlike most others—is interested in everything. I admire this enthusiasm—the zeal with which he approaches an exhibition, or the interest he takes in new publications. He is determined to take in the world and follow as much of it as possible. When new and promising figures emerge in the art world—as happens relatively often—he does everything he can to make contact with them. And so, should he fail to say a single word about my text, despite his open and receptive nature, this speaks volumes: he considers it to be either unworthy of discussion or so questionable that he would rather not mention it at all. When we meet, I swear time and again that I will not force a reaction from him; that is, that I will not under any circumstances ask for his opinion regarding my texts. Should he fail to mention them himself, I sit there as if frozen. I am left wondering if I can really assume the existence of a potential readership when even one of my closest friends seems to have no interest in my work.

Admittedly, the notion that I am surrounded by disinterest is hopelessly self-pitying and paranoid. There are of course people in my immediate circle who follow my work with interest, and who offer me their private or public support. And in writing this book on friendship, my hope is that it reaches not only my friends but also readers unknown to me, who might see their own social circles reflected in it. If I took the pessimistic view that my observations will inevitably fall on deaf ears, I would hardly make the effort to write them down at all. Nor is it the case that there is no one within my circle whom I can trust to give me their honest critical opinion on this manuscript; on the contrary, I have a few close friends whom I am consulting throughout the project. Nothing I write will be published without them reading it first. For they have my protection in mind.

**8.20.2020**

But in giving this manuscript to a friend, I put them in a difficult position. On the one hand, I draw them into the logic of the useful friendship: they do something for me, and I benefit from their input. On the other, there is a risk that they will see the book as a reflection on our own relationship—as a representation of it, with the potential to offend. They may feel I have located them within a hierarchical social structure without affording them a voice of their own. In this light, it seems advisable that I hand over the manuscript to only a few people, and always with the appropriate warning. I am also considering asking my daughter to publish it posthumously, which would spare me a great deal of aggravation.

Writing this book away from the usual channels of feedback is a consequence of the pandemic. My current lifestyle is a highly reclusive one. The lack of any external stimuli—shared dinners, talks, conferences—means I must generate the motivation for this project alone, which I find exhausting. A friendly-minded agent would make all the difference here—someone to hold me to deadlines and push me to finish the book. There is no immediate prospect of any such support, but I push forward anyway with energy and enthusiasm (and sometimes obstinacy), in the hope that my thoughts on friendship will interest someone or other.

**8.21.2020**

It seems appropriate at this point to draw a more differentiated picture of my friendships. In times of "misfortune" (as Arendt puts it)—such as the sudden deaths of my parents—I did experience great care and compassion from some friends. In the initial period of paralyzing shock, especially, this support often came from those whom I would not necessarily have expected to show such empathy. Others, by contrast, unsure how to deal with my desolate state, or with experiences of death more generally, backed away from me somewhat; the misfortune I suffered thus had the effect of reordering my friendships.

Having experienced true friendship in my times of weakness and need, I see the more instrumental friendships in my life in a new light. My expectations of friendship are now different, which is not only due to the crises and losses of recent years but also a result of getting older. While shared political and aesthetic ideals and the mutual pursuit of our careers were the driving forces of some earlier friendships, I now value caring qualities in my friends more highly than I once did.

Seen from this perspective, the number of my true friends shrinks considerably. There are only a few who show real care, whereas the list of formerly personal relationships that have now become friendly professional ones—but which are not friendships in the emphatic sense—is long. Just a few years ago, I believed I had a great number of friends, but I can now count my true friends on one hand. All others are essentially partners in some shared venture or other.

This may sound like an exaggeration, but it reflects the reality of the situation. It is also supported by the recent comments of an old acquaintance, an artist who—incidentally—now earns a lot of money from her paintings. After I told her about my friendship project, she surprised me by stating that she believes she has no friends, that there is no one she can turn to or put her trust in in times of need. Instead, she is surrounded by acquaintances, comrades, and companions—a set of people that also renews itself completely every ten years. According to her, friendships have a limited shelf life within the art world and are subject to regular periodic changes according to the social status, career situations, and personal preferences of those involved.

I do not mean to lament lost illusions about friendship here. In fact, I am happy I now know whom I can really count on; there is little reason to fear any of these few true friends dropping me at the first opportunity, or betraying me. It's important to point out that such betrayals are not unusual in highly competitive situations such as that of the art world; on the contrary, to weaken and attack one's peers by speaking badly of their work is actively encouraged. Only in a few cases do I feel sure that someone would never speak of me in this way.

**8.22.2020**

That real, non-instrumentalized friendships are currently facing difficulties and new challenges is due in part to certain social factors that extend into my own private friendship dramas. The notion of personal responsibility is constantly praised within neoliberal economies, reinforcing the idea that people are to blame for their own failures. This is not exactly conducive to friendship, especially since even critical spirits are not immune to the mantra that we are each individually accountable for our actions. Intellectuals, too (and I include myself here), can sometimes end up placing some of the responsibility for their friends' crises and misfortunes on the people involved, despite them being largely a result of social conditions. For individual action and social structures are mutually interrelated in "failure," with the inextricable influence of several different factors making it difficult to determine the portion of responsibility to be taken for one's own actions. This is made even more difficult by the fact that there are no objective criteria for what is considered failure: situations that some experience as failures can seem wholly desirable to others. And in addition to all those who follow the cult of success within the art world, there are others who consciously avoid career pressures in order to prioritize their work's content or political aspects.

At some point—generally in their fifties—even those who have long resisted market success tend to do all they can to earn more money and avoid slipping into poverty in their later years. Most of my friends do aspire to a "good life," with comfortable living conditions and regular vacations. But to realize such a lifestyle has become increasingly expensive, meaning complaints about high living costs, low rates of pay, self-exploitation, and a lack of institutional recognition are commonplace in conversations with my closer art-world friends. Some tend to see their lives as only ever drawing a negative balance, blaming their situations on everyone but themselves. As well informed as I may be about the structural dimensions of their failures (and my own), I sometimes catch myself thinking that they might also have contributed to their own misery. And the more space I give to this thought, the less inclined I am to help these friends when they fall into difficulties—not just emotionally, but by supporting them financially, for example.

The philosopher Arne Johan Vetlesen recently pointed out that the social discourse around responsibility serves to single us out (which goes against the ideal of friendship). If each of us is made responsible for our own situation, this isolates us from one another. This separation must then be overcome for friendships to form, meaning the isolating discourse of responsibility hinders friendship even at the level of its formation. Society leaves us to fend for ourselves, which makes us reluctant to really engage with others. It makes a crucial difference whether we give in to or resist this pressure to isolate ourselves—by ensuring we still come together with others. But the power of these forces cannot be underestimated; they may simply be too strong and too pervasive to be resisted by any one individual.

**8.23.2020**

An additional problem is the lack of time that the constant obligation for responsible self-management produces. This deficit of time that could potentially be spent on others is a further obstacle to friendship: isolated from one another, we are occupied by the administration of our lives, with barely any room left over for our friends. The resource of time is central to friendships, and it is increasingly scarce. I now have to plan meetings with my friends far in advance, often even weeks ahead, as we scour our diaries together for a gap in our schedules. Spontaneous phone calls have also become a rarity since the other person is often busy, and any call is planned well ahead of time.

To actively care for one's friendships is not easy in a situation of permanent professional overload; there simply isn't the time. And yet we need our friendships now more than ever, in part because of the erosion of earlier social forms that once supported us, such as family and extended kinship. Sociologists like Janosch Schobin see friendship under these conditions as a "caring social form" whose rise has been partly fueled by the collapse of the welfare state; today, it is friendships that adopt the caring role that was once the preserve of social welfare systems. Seen from this perspective, the ideal of caring friendship is entirely in keeping with the logic of a capitalist system that dismantles the social functions of the state and outsources them to private interests.

The great hopes currently placed on friendship are matched by the new social challenges it faces. While I foster no illusions about a friendship ever being entirely free of self-interest, I also pursue just that: friendships free of self-interest. There are friends to whom I give a great deal without keeping a tally of whether or not I've received enough from them in return. And yet I also wonder if true friendship, in the Aristotelian sense, where the other is valued for "their own sake," is possible at all among art-world friends. Even the mythical friendships between nineteenth- and twentieth-century artists, such as the close bond between Van Gogh and Gauguin, can clearly be seen to have been primarily instrumental; those involved in such friendships sought to benefit from each other artistically. I suspect many such relationships exist among the artists of today, driven by a mutual desire to profit from one another in artistic terms. There are structural reasons for this, which I will relate tomorrow.

**8.24.2020**

While artist friendships are a prime example of friendly relationships with an instrumental streak, the entire art business might be described as being conducted in a mode of friendship. The collectors, curators, artists, critics, and others who interact within this world often relate to one another as friends, or at the very least purport to be friends with one another. On the one hand, this has many benefits, as I myself know from experience: it's far easier to get what I want from someone if I know them personally. Often, a (friendly) earlier working relationship means I already have the number of the person in question saved in my phone; my old address books from the 1990s—now practically falling apart—contain the names of many colleagues who were unknown back then but now belong to the who's who of the art world. The friendly approach also makes it easier to talk openly among friends, and to come directly to the point. For as with so-called business friends, those involved in the art business get a better feel for their business partners if they are also friends. Anchored within this is the principle that "one hand washes the other": anyone who does me a favor is due one in return, and is bound to call it in at some point in the future.

As a critic, I have benefited hugely from being active in this milieu since the late 1980s, meaning I now have access to a wide network of friendly working relationships. The informal deals that are typical of the art world can be far more effectively agreed upon between quasi friends, since the usual need for caution is minimized. Without the bonds of friendship greasing the wheels of art-world deals, the informal nature of its economy would be unimaginable, and it is this culture of trust that enables an otherwise unregulated field to be governed by unwritten laws. Business relationships such as those between an artist and their gallerist, for example, are not usually contractual; what counts far more are verbal agreements made between parties who communicate through the mode of friendship.

While there are downsides to personal transactions of this type, such as nontransparency and an absence of legal protection, an informal economy without contracts makes it easier to achieve one's goals free of the usual bureaucracy. That the lack of regulation in the art world opens up many possibilities is what first attracted me to it, and what has inspired and fascinated me—and also entertained me—in the time since. A quasi friendship yields quick agreements and speedy results that can sometimes be a great pleasure. But for all the opportunities this system offers, and for all its seeming openness, it is also responsible for upholding the art milieu's exclusive character and rigid barriers to entry. Should someone fail to demonstrate the cosmopolitan habits on which the art world's friendships are built, they are likely to remain outside of it. And due to its informal unregulated economy, the art world is also prone to abuses of power—as many of the recent #MeToo cases in this milieu have demonstrated.

**8.25.2020**

Friendship is a "practice of trust" (as the philosopher Martin Hartmann puts it), but not everyone is afforded the confidence it requires. According to Hartmann, we generally prefer those who are at home within the "same institutional regime" as ourselves, meaning anyone who is from a different class or cultural background may be treated with more suspicion. I myself have observed how trust develops more easily between those of similar backgrounds. For a long time, there were only a few people with personal or family histories of migration in my circle of friends and acquaintances. Thankfully, this is now changing, in part as a consequence of social protest movements like Black Lives Matter. People who feel themselves to be somehow marked as "other" now rightly insist to be included, while my colleagues and I now feel we have a responsibility to ensure there is more diversity within our field—a diversity that is not merely cosmetic but implies a change in power structures. At the same time, friendship is not something that can be forced, and it ultimately needs an intellectual or emotional basis in order to succeed. To find this commonality with someone who is socially marked or positioned differently to oneself takes active effort. Friendships do not form of their own accord.

However, even the most heterogeneous network of professional friends can prove problematic if one never escapes it. This was my own experience for many years: I didn't know anyone who wasn't somehow located within the art world, and I had no alternative to this scene. Every one of my social interactions carried its DNA, and there seemed to be no escape from its milieu. I have since succeeded in accessing other circles, and I do now have friends outside the art world. Any related business is left at the door in these relationships—to my own benefit and that of the friendships themselves.

The emphatically friendly manner that is cultivated among the members of the art world also seems to me to stem from the unique qualities of its product: artworks. It is precisely because artworks are a special type of commodity—one whose enormous symbolic value means it can never be reduced to its price alone—that the trade in them has the appearance of a friendly exchange.

**8.26.2020**

While the culture of friendliness in the art world demonstrates that art should ideally be about more than mere economic calculations, these friendly interactions are also business oriented. It's for this reason that the artist Andrea Fraser once fittingly described them as examples of "transactional friendships"—business relationships cloaked in the mantle of friendship. Like business relationships, transactional friendships aim to profit from the other person; if there is nothing more to be gained from the transactional friend, the connection usually melts away. As with "useful friendships" that at some point cease to be useful, a transactional friendship has no reason to exist beyond the transaction itself. Such friendships are clearly far from the Aristotelian ideal of true, unselfish friendship; here, the other person is valued not for their own sake but for what they bring to the transaction.

And yet Aristotle's vision of valuing a friend entirely for who they are also strikes me as hopelessly outdated. I myself find it difficult to draw a clear line between the "real me," for which I hope to be valued by others, and my career activities. Are my texts, talks, and books not also part of who I am? Are there aspects of my personality that still make me worthy of friendship independent of my work—like friendliness, amiability, and compassion? While I naturally hope to be valued for such qualities by my closest friends, I would never demand they show me friendship while ignoring my professional activities entirely. In the sphere of art and culture especially, people tend to define themselves through their work. To attempt to peel away someone's career and find the independent and friendship-worthy "essence" within seems to me to be futile under these conditions.

**8.27.2020**

It is not only the transformation of friendships into transactions that is putting them under strain. The fluid boundary between collaborators and competitors in our network economy also makes nurturing friendships difficult; not only do I work with certain friends, but our relationship to each other is also one of competition. The theater-studies scholar Kai van Eikels fittingly speaks of "co-competition" in this context, describing the tendency for cooperation and competition to merge, above all within collective projects—although a distinction should be drawn here betweenproductive, stimulating competition and destructive rivalry. While competing with another person can sometimes be motivating, the negative fixation on a supposed rival can have a self-destructive dimension. The likelihood that what starts off as a friendly competition will at some point tip over into bitter rivalry is also high; it can even be the case that long-term friends and colleagues suddenly reveal themselves to be "frenemies." Friend and foe collapse into one person in such cases, meaning it is advisable to approach the person in question with suspicion. Not infrequently, I have been forced to realize that someone I considered a friend had long been plotting my downfall, perhaps without them even knowing it.

To openly thematize such aggressive but unconscious desires is tantamount to breaking a taboo. I once confronted a colleague with my impression that, for all his rhetoric of solidarity, he was actually seeking to damage me professionally. His response—most likely because it was an unconscious act on his part—was one of burning indignation. Negative feelings like hate or envy are simply not allowed, despite them being unavoidable in any competitive society. No one is immune to them. Naturally it stings when a friend and colleague publishes more than I do or receives more recognition for her work, even if I am at the same time genuinely happy for her. So while negative feelings are undeniably present in any situation of competition, only rarely have I experienced them being directly addressed within a friendship.

In this context, I recall a situation where a friend and I were competing for the same grant. We discussed in advance what effect it might have on our friendship were only one of us to receive the funding, and we swore to remain friends in spite of this, and to celebrate the other's success—we were determined not to let a competitive situation drive a wedge into our friendship. We mutually supported and advised each other throughout the application process. Things turned out happily, and we were both successful. The fact that we had confronted the situation and its potential consequences for our relationship served to consolidate the bond between us. If the pressure to compete within a friendship is addressed by those involved, there is a chance it will survive and continue. Moreover, in ideal cases, to be able to negotiate negative affects such as envy and rivalry can even deepen a friendship.

**8.28.2020**

An even harder test of the "friendship principle" has come from social media, where every contact has the status of a "friend." A large proportion of these friends is, in reality, made up of distant acquaintances or people with whom one has no personal relationship at all, which ultimately amounts to a hollowing out of the concept of friendship itself. And yet the greater the number of these contacts that have taken the form of "friends" on Facebook, the higher my network capital.

These Facebook friends are naturally a long way from those true friends who have stood by me in times of personal upheaval; a "friend" is no longer really a friend in the context of social media, and the word loses its original meaning of a close and trusted confidant. It would be interesting to examine the effects of this altered notion of friendship on our real-world social lives. Is the indifference we feel toward most of our online friends carried over to those offline? Or is the reverse the case, with the inflation caused by our online pseudo friendships making the analog experience of meeting others in person a more valuable commodity?

If any random person can now be declared to be a friend, then friendship loses its exclusive character. To me this represents both a loss and a gain: friendship loses its potential for an exclusive bond and friends become arbitrary and exchangeable. For if anyone can be my friend, there is no longer any need to exclude those who are not my friends. At the same time, friendship itself becomes more accessible and inclusive. Friendship with me is now theoretically open to everyone—it is only the final narrow threshold separating "friends" from "followers" that still needs to be overcome. On the other hand, does this diminished exclusivity not equally diminish the very point of friendship? For if it really is to be had with everyone, then its fundamental character—as something that is unique and specific—is lost.

**8.29.2020**

It is precisely because friendship has become increasingly prone to disruption both online and offline that the desire for it is so pronounced. This is my own experience: I long for my friends more than ever, and I value them more than ever. With the end of every friendship, the part of me that I only ever acted out with that person goes missing. It is not only the friend in question whom I must mourn when our friendship dies, but also this lost part of myself, leaving me feeling as if a part of me has been amputated. As the number of my friendships that have broken apart for one reason or another increases, my remaining friends are increasingly close to my heart. I take care to maintain close contact with them, and I hope that we will accompany each other throughout the highs and lows of our lives.

For Aristotle, the duration of a friendship was the fundamental measure of its quality; according to him, it is only those with whom we hold long-term bonds who can be described as our true friends. But for a friendship to be sustained over time entails the reality of death: it is inevitable that one friend or the other will eventually die, likely leaving the other behind. Seen in this light, true friendship also means staying loyal to someone even when they are no longer alive. Apropos death, I sometimes find myself envisaging the eulogies I will one day deliver at the graves of my closest friends. I resolve that our connection will not end with their deaths, and that I will keep it alive in my words and thoughts. For it is entirely down to the surviving friend to determine whether the friendship remains full of life posthumously or not.

The rifts I have experienced with my friends carry consequences that extend beyond the grave. Even the occasion of their funerals might one day cause me to torture myself with the question of whether my presence is desired or appropriate. Is it acceptable to say goodbye to someone you no longer had any contact with? And how will they behave at my funeral—will they stay away or attempt some sort of posthumous reconciliation by attending? Thankfully, these questions do not currently apply. I continue to live, as do all my friends and ex-friends.

That duration alone determines whether a friendship is true and thus "good" was also the opinion of Albert Camus. In a 1943 letter to his colleague Francis Ponge, he writes that "there are friendships that last and others that do not. Those that last are good friendships—it is very simple." He therefore distinguished between good friendships, which endure, and all others, which do not, and are thus inferior. In my view, the reality is less straightforward. Had I, in the spirit of Camus, failed to believe in the potential for good and enduring bonds in my many broken friendships—including the numerous semi-instrumental relationships of my Cologne years—would I have entered into them at all? Is it not rather the case that our needs are subject to situational changes, and that altered conditions cause friends to appear under a new light? A friendship once experienced as fulfilling and enlivening can seem harmful and onerous in different circumstances—while it once offered me something, in a different context it feels like a burden. I felt deep affection for the numerous friends I made in Cologne in the 1990s, and it would be wrong to devalue this feeling in retrospect and dismiss it as an illusion.

Back when I was younger and more driven by ambition, shared intellectual interests and aspirations were pivotal in forming social alliances. Having grown older, however, it is the caring aspect of friendship that is more important to me. Above all, I now seek to offer my friends emotional and social support. Any bonds that were primarily instrumental have, by contrast, loosened. But this does not mean that my instrumental friendships were not genuine. It simply never would have occurred to me to trouble such people with my emotions—it was more important to me that we shared an ethos.

**8.30.2020**

I do however find it uncomfortable when friends from my youth to whom I have long held no connection make sudden demands for friendship. They contact me as if it were the most natural thing to do so; as if no time had passed at all since our last meeting, which feels to me as if it happened a hundred years ago. Out of nowhere, they bring up things we once shared but which I have long since forgotten. They talk to me as if I'm the same person I used to be, without having changed in the time since. With an insistence that can sometimes feel overbearing, they do everything they can to act as if I were still the person they once knew. If I attempt to resist their violent efforts to pigeonhole me, they barely register it; to them, I'm just the same old me. At a recent party, I happened to bump into a fellow student from my time in Paris; he instantly began referring to me by my old nickname ("Frau Frida," the generic moniker for a German woman), attempting to pin me down to the image he had formed of me back then. He continually brought up our earlier familiarity, ignoring the fact that it had not existed for some time. I felt this to be invasive, and so I attempted to withdraw myself from the situation.

Nietzsche once made a mean-spirited but enlightening comment on this phenomenon, claiming that our former friends appear as "ghosts of our pasts" in such encounters. They force us into a confrontation with our younger selves, who were "more severe" and "less mature"—identities that we believe ourselves to have long outgrown. I am well accustomed to the sense of being reduced to a (supposed) earlier identity, as with the encounter with the acquaintance from my student days. But Nietzsche's arrogant pose also seems questionable to me, since it assumes that he, unlike his friends, has continued to develop. At the same time, the reverse could easily be true: that his friends see him as never having moved on, even though he sees himself as having outgrown them. Perhaps it is precisely those people who, like Nietzsche, assume their old friends are stuck in a sort of arrested development that are themselves treading water. So when a friend from my student days insists on acting as if it were still 1984, I must at least consider the possibility that he sees me as being tragically stuck in the past myself. "Development" among friends is also never objective: while one friend may consider herself to be totally transformed, the other may perceive her as being entirely unchanged.

**8.31.2020**

Janosch Schobin states that conversation is the central practice of friendship. It is in talking with our friends, he argues, that their "caring and supportive" presence manifests itself; here, the company of another proves to be healing. It's true that it is hard to imagine a friendship without conversation; indeed, it's only when talking to a friend that I really experience the benefit of our relationship. And yet their behavior in such situations can sometimes demonstrate the deficits or boundaries that exist within a friendship. During a recent discussion with Dorothee, an old friend of mine, I came to realize how unfriendly her behavior toward me has become. She told me outright that our friendship would have to come to an end due to our political conflicts, since the most important thing to her was to avoid falling out with those whose political views she shared. The idea that our friendship could survive our political disagreements on how to critique liberalism from a radical left position was not an option for her. Her own career was—as she openly admitted—more important to her than our friendship; my convictions that some liberal inventions like "critique" had to be updated and defended meant I had now become an enemy in her eyes. She didn't seem concerned about the impact her aggressive words could have on me. And yet it took this conversation to wake me up to the fact that our friendship had gone to waste; listening to her speak, I realized

I could no longer count her among my friends. Conversations are rituals from which we might just as equally deduce the end of a friendship as experience its special qualities.

What characterizes friendly conversations is, Schobin claims, an exchange of secrets. By mutually entrusting our friends with our confidences, we grant them a sort of symbolic collateral regarding our private lives. It's true that sharing secrets with someone in this way means surrendering oneself to them and offering them something that is fundamentally one's own. Any such exchange generally requires trust.

I have recently observed how confidential or personal information can sometimes be disclosed outside of such situations of trust, with the intimate culture of conversation between friends now having forced its way into our interactions with those we don't know. The readiness to trust strangers or distant acquaintances has increased among my women friends especially, and I have noticed the same tendency within myself: to open up too quickly to strangers, almost immediately informing them of the details of my personal situation. I recently met a woman on the beach, and after an hour of conversation, I knew more about her and she more about me than our closest friends do. Could this be an unfulfilled desire for intimate personal contact, making its voice heard in the wrong place? Or is it the very distance to this woman that emboldened me, and her, to speak so freely? After all, we did not have to fear the other instantly divulging our secrets to our mutual acquaintainces, a fear that would be more justified with our friends. Interestingly, this problem of indiscretion among friends goes unmentioned in Schobin's observations.

And yet even our good friends cannot be assumed to keep the secrets we entrust them with to themselves. Nietzsche was under no illusions in this respect. In his view, there are few people who would not immediately divulge "the more private affairs of their friends," particularly if they need "material for conversation." Anyone who wants to make a valuable contribution to a conversation with a friend, then, shares a secret that was entrusted to them elsewhere. Even close friends might break a confidence in the right situation—that much Nietzsche likely had right. In fact, it is highly probable that what was entrusted to them will eventually be passed on to someone else.

But in my experience, there is more at stake in such social indiscretions than the mere desire to have something to say. If I repeat something told to me in confidence (always under the pledge of secrecy, of course), then in doing so, I also acknowledge the value of such information within my economy, the art world. By passing on this gossip to others, I put myself at an advantage: since I now know more than my conversation partner, I can adapt more quickly than her to the changed situation this knowledge brings. Gossip is therefore also the expression of a competitive advantage that arms one for the future.

At the same time, by conveying a message that was supposed to remain a secret, I demonstrate to my counterpart that I enjoy privileged access to my source of information. With this, the circle closes, since any such access is generally due to a trusting and sociable relationship with the person involved, which I also demonstrate through my indiscretion. I therefore flaunt my trusting relationship with the source of the information at the very moment I betray this trust.

**9.1.2020**

Friendships also live from what remains unsaid within them, as my friend Christian pointed out to me yesterday after I had given him the previous pages of this manuscript to read. He objected to my dragging into the light what is usually hidden, and above all to how I have chosen to do so. He also felt uncomfortable at seeing himself made into a pawn on the chessboard of my friendships, without me having discussed this with him in advance. And yet I never had him in mind when developing any of my characters! His vehement reaction to my draft shocked me. I realized that by giving voice to what usually goes unspoken in friendships, I was endangering not only my relationship with Christian but all my friendships. Maintaining the stability of these bonds requires that much that relates to them directly is not mentioned and remains in the shadows.

For the sake of these friendships, might it not be better to take the opposite approach and limit myself to vague insinuations instead?

I resolved to make the figures in question less familiar, particularly since my interest is not in describing specific people, and certainly not in locating them within my friendship network. Instead, my aim is to demonstrate how the current pressures of our competitive society extend into our relationships with our friends—in part by examining fictionalized experiences from my own life. It is precisely because my friendships are also shaped by social structures that they may be compared, despite the unique nature of each.

As unexpected as it may seem, I would also like to pay tribute at this point to my inimitable friends Majorie and Solange. I first met Solange in the late 1990s during regular meetings with colleagues at a café in Cologne. She has mastered the art of friendship like no other, as can be seen from the fact that she remains close to a friend from her early childhood. From the very beginning, she showed a degree of kindness and support that I had otherwise never experienced. While she may appear somewhat stern and unapproachable at first, in reality she is extremely receptive to other people and their problems. We have each gotten into the habit of sending the other a text message every morning to check how they are, ensuring that neither of us ever feels alone.

I have known Majorie since my elementary school days, and we sat next to each other in high school. She helped me when I struggled with mathematics, and I corrected her essays for our German classes. While she took a very different path to my own in her career and private life—she is a lawyer and lives on a farm near Hamburg with her husband and four children—we still have a close bond. Her face is the friendliest and freshest I know. She, too, places great value on her friendships, especially since the early death of her sister, and she puts loyalty to her friends above everything else. In times of emergency, Majorie will drop everything and hurry to a friend who is struggling or needs help. I will never forget how she once picked me up from the main station in Hamburg after I had gone through a painful breakup. I had told her how hard it was for me to arrive in a city where no one was waiting for me—and there she was.

Majorie and Solange each afford their friends a central place in their lives, which is not always easy for their partners, who at times feel relegated to second place instead of getting priority treatment. Indeed, Majorie and Solange do spend a lot of time immersing themselves in their friends' emotional lives, offering them words of reassurance and encouragement in times of doubt. Solange especially looks for structures that go beyond the individual, which I find to be an enormous help and comfort; to realize that some of the humiliations I face are in part an expression of sexist structures within society means I do not have to take them upon myself to the same extent. We are also able to laugh about the dramas we each experience in our personal crises.

Both Majorie and Solange show me a special kind of sympathy. They take an active interest in my life, enveloping me in their friendship. They have carried me through periods of upheaval that were greatly unsettling, such as separations from partners or the deaths of my parents. Their affection can be read in their every word and gesture, and this allows me to be a little more forgiving of myself; it's as if the empathy they show rubs off and causes me to judge myself less harshly. Without their coaching, I don't know how I would have survived the numerous crises throughout my life. By letting me know that my happiness is important to them, they ensure I am not lost to myself, which helps me find my footing. And by addressing my experiences, they also signal that these are deserving of their interest and attention; that the things that happen to me are not unimportant, even if this depressing thought does sometimes occur to me. The advice they offer is never intrusive or presumptuous; any suggestions are carefully formulated and do not gloss over the substantive differences in our respective situations. After discussing the nuts and bolts of my private life with them, it is usually easier for me to address these problems myself. Viewed from their less despondent perspective, these problems seem manageable; I am left feeling emboldened, filled with new hope. The depressing feeling that my personal situation is of no importance evaporates the moment Solange or Majorie engages with it.

As soon as I am faced with existential decisions—whether of a professional or private nature—I ask for their advice. It's no exaggeration to say that the most consequential decisions I have made in my life can be traced back to their support. Without their encouragement, I would not have finished writing my dissertation or dared have a child despite the demands of my work. At the same time, they have taken a critical view of some of my life decisions—compromises that I make for the sake of money, for example. Solange especially is forthright with her thoughts, but knowing she has my best interests at heart means I am happy to take her advice. She allows me to take the wrong path occasionally, gently pointing out my mistakes and steering me back on course. Even my deepest fears (first among them my well-known fear of abandonment) are easier to cope with when I can share them with Majorie and Solange. To unload my burdens and oppressions with them immediately lightens the weight of my suffering; by making them a "problem shared" (as is so often said), they become tolerable.

**9.2.2020**

What effects do class differences have on my close friendships, I wonder? Do they prevent real intimacy from developing, or does the intensity of our affection mean our relationships transcend such distinctions? In *Returning to Reims*, Didier Eribon describes class differences as undermining friendships. Even the most intimate bonds, he claims, will at some point lead to an irreconcilable standoff when held between friends of different classes, a result of either their negligence or their deeply ingrained habits. Those from middle-class backgrounds, for example, tend to assume that everyone else—including their working-class friends—shares the same cultural experiences as themselves. Comments that are intended to be entirely free of aggression may therefore be experienced as hurtful by someone from a different milieu.

I find Eribon's description of the symbolic violence of

class affiliation to be entirely fitting, and there is no doubt that this violence can be a cause of pain within friendships. I am however skeptical of his economic determinism and tendency to essentialize the relationship between class and habit. It may be true that some of my friends feel my fluent French or familiarity with Baroque music (both of which I acquired as a child) are privileges that were denied them in their own childhoods. But our habits are never entirely straightforward—there is usually some sort of split in our behavior. Just as I was strongly shaped by my parents' upper-middle-class cultural identity, I also grew up in more modest conditions following their divorce. So while I can perform the role of the "well-bred" young woman, I simultaneously view myself through the eyes of a left-wing intellectual who feels anything but at home among the staid and sated bourgeoisie.

This has a twofold effect on my friendships with those from less privileged backgrounds. I might insensitively assume that ballet classes and violin lessons are desirable and affordable for all children, but I also maintain a distance from those aspirational parents who come together in ballet school and take their privileges for granted, considering themselves to be deserving of them. For me, bourgeois culture is connected with a presumed self-confidence that, in reality, has a brittle facade. The more cracks that appear in this facade—in the form of stereotypically middle-class fears about the potential loss of status, for example—the more doggedly it is upheld.

My love of staging multiple class identities also extends into my friendship with Solange, who has a less well-off background than my own and takes great pleasure in enacting bourgeois rituals. But while I am able to let go of their protocols and codes of conduct once in a while and just relax with my feet up on the table, to stage a dinner without a tablecloth would be unthinkable for her. It is in these moments that the class differences between us become the most apparent: when I nonchalantly abandon those bourgeois conventions she upholds so rigidly, in part since she had to work hard to learn them. The good thing, however, is that we can discuss the differences our respective backgrounds produce in our lives.

By talking about the effects of our class identities on our self-understanding, we might prevent the sort of irritations Eribon describes from emerging between us.

In his book *Changer: méthode*, Édouard Louis describes the history of his life as a sequence of broken friendships. He shows how he was forced to separate himself from those he once loved in order to move forward. He made targeted use of his friends in his social ascension, taking in their bourgeois rituals and self-assured manner and learning them for himself. But the fact that he wanted to advance even further meant he had to leave them behind; they did not share in his development, which caused a gulf to emerge between them. The instrumental aspect of friendship proves to be a necessity born of class in this account: anyone who, like Louis, seeks to escape their working-class milieu at any cost can do so only via others—their friends—since it is they who hold the key to social distinction. Having successfully learned the ways of the bourgeois lifestyle, Louis then moved on.

I do not share his entirely instrumental view of friendship. For even if the bonds with his friends were subordinated to a higher purpose—his social advancement—they were also based on other factors, like his affection for or interest in the people in question. Nonetheless, it is striking that Louis considers change to be something that can only be effected through one's friends. His "method" is that of friendship: friends are the generators and catalysts of the changes in his personality. Without orienting himself in relation to them, he would have been unable to rise above the conditions of the class of his birth.

**9.3.2020**

In my own life, there have been friendships that were unable to withstand the divergent life paths of those involved. If one friend makes the decision to have a family and children, for example, while the other continues her single lifestyle, this can cause irritations that range from the minor to the severe. When I had a child some years ago, it was not easy for some of my friends to adapt to my altered reality. As a mother, I was no longer constantly available for shared activities—whether visiting exhibitions or going out—and making plans with me became more complicated. Since I frequently stayed away from social occasions such as exhibition openings, I was also no longer informed about what happened at these events, which I would otherwise have debated and discussed with friends later on. These conversations were a central ritual of the collusion between us, which was now endangered by their absence. And yet I preferred to stay home in order to spend time with my young daughter—nocturnal excursions to bars and restaurants no longer brought me as much pleasure as they once had. At the same time, I could afford to forgo my social life and the networking opportunities it provided, which surely made it far easier for me to make this choice. My professional life was thankfully rather stable at the time of my daughter's birth, and so the threat my social retreat posed was far less severe than it would have been earlier in my life. I was considered a "geriatric pregnancy," as the ageist term for my situation describes it, and I had already built something of a nest for myself. Despite this, however, my absence still ran the risk of removing me from the stages where art-world friendships play out; after all, it is at events like openings or dinners that they are visibly performed for all to see.

My relationships with my childless women friends were especially clouded by underlying tensions at times. The decision not to have children does not have to be a sacrifice, and it need not involve sadness or pain. But should an inner confrontation regarding this decision not take place, unprocessed and potentially painful emotions can sometimes express themselves as latent feelings of aggression or envy toward a friend with a child. This envy does not show itself directly, however; according to the psychoanalyst Horst Petri, it manifests itself as an inability to relate. I repeatedly experienced a variant of this lack of empathy: there were friends who barely concealed their disinterest in my daughter, and whose attention faded to indifference as soon as I spoke of her. If a child is not given a place within a friendship, then this—Petri claims—produces "grievous gaps within the feeling of friendship." I could tell you a thing or two about such grievous gaps. I remember being visited at home by one friend, a curator whose company I had previously enjoyed greatly and often. She sat down at the kitchen table, directly next to the spot where my then two-year-old daughter sat in her high chair. While my child tried in numerous ways to get her attention (by crying and throwing objects), she resolutely persisted in telling me of art-world matters; she completely ignored the situation I now found myself in as the mother of a whining child. I finished this meeting as quickly as I could, since it was irreconcilable with my new living situation.

Another long-term colleague of mine, a fellow critic, insisted on always meeting me alone following the birth of my daughter. She preferred to wait for the days I was "free," when my daughter was with her father, rather than visit me at home when she was also there. In this, I saw her technique for avoiding being confronted with the presence of my child. Her denial of the person who had become the most important in my life was quite hurtful. A process of alienation set in between us, and we now have barely anything to do with one another. I could understand the difficulties she had adapting to my altered situation; it must have been painful for her, too, to see my priorities shift toward my child, who now came first. But in my eyes, it would have been helpful if she had addressed the problems she felt my new role as a mother brought with it, instead of insisting on meeting me alone, which I refused to do.

**9.4.2020**

While I greatly enjoyed the time at home with my daughter, I was occasionally overcome with fears that I might be "missing out"; I worried that my friendships and social contacts would drop away entirely. At the same time, there were (and are) good friends of mine who adapted very well to my new lifestyle. When making plans, they don't mind if they have to adapt to my tight schedule. One close friend even repeatedly offered her services as a babysitter in order to give me some time for myself and my work. Her consideration and willingness to help touched me greatly, and my affection for her grew as a result. She would also keep me up to date on things I had missed, which made me feel less excluded. The balance sheet of my friendships since becoming a mother is therefore far from being entirely negative.

I have also made new friends through my daughter, including the parents of other children at her kindergarten or school. Such friendships are themselves not free of utility, of course, since they are based on mutual support and advice regarding school or parenting problems. But the fact that we, as parents, do not usually have any shared career interests means these friendships can be relatively straightforward and unselfish. We help and support each other without expecting it to benefit our careers. The other parents do not offer any immediate advantage in my professional life, even if knowing them personally can, naturally, represent a "gain" in a world based on such contacts. In view of the neoliberal ideal of a broad and diversified network of friends, such friendships between parents are worth their weight in gold. For it is through them that one might potentially open the door to social and professional spheres that would otherwise remain closed off.

**9.5.2020**

While my friendships with other parents have proven to be remarkably stable (although this might change as my daughter approaches the end of her time at school), some of my friendships with artists have collapsed. It's hard for me to reconstruct what it was that caused them to break apart; sometimes it was due to new partners I was unable to warm to—while my friends, in turn, probably experienced something similar—or else we simply drifted away from each other as a consequence of our different worldviews.

When two artist friends retreated from the art world, for example, I considered this to be a strategic mistake. I could understand their desire to seek shelter from its hard-edged and relentlessly competitive culture. But since I myself had resolved to continue facing it head-on, and wanted to succeed in doing so, the realities of our lives diverged. At first we had less to do with each other, and then at some point nothing at all. In my view, they placed themselves in an (imaginary) position "outside" of things, which did not have a positive effect on their work.

Other art-world friendships of mine failed on account of irreconcilable political differences. Following the election of Donald Trump, I found it particularly hard to deal with those artist friends who doggedly stuck to their libertarian identities as transgressive bohemian types who flout all the rules. Their freedom to break with social conventions, especially, was something they were not willing to concede; they insisted on remaining damaged subjects, capable of openly lying and other pathological behavior if they felt it was necessary. But to subscribe to such an idea of freedom has a very different meaning in the Trump era; to ignore all rules and act recklessly is his brand, after all. His abandonment of the usual social norms has an antidemocratic thrust, and is usually at the expense of other (weaker) people. One must therefore draw a distinction between dubious rule-breaking in the Trumpian mold and defensible nonconformist artistic strategies that aim at a necessary break with certain dominant conventions.

And yet the liberties that were once taken by macho artist-provocateurs such as Sigmar Polke and Martin Kippenberger must now be viewed in a different light, as some of my freedom-loving friends refuse to accept. They complain that there is nothing at all one is still allowed to say, thus picking up (often unconsciously) on a right-wing topos that constantly invokes the imagined hegemony of "political correctness." This bears no relation to reality; on the contrary, far-right party members and coronavirus deniers are free to broadcast their opinions to the world as much as they like. If an artist friend tells me they are no longer prepared to follow the linguistic rules that are supposedly restricting their work, I try to explain that there were good reasons for establishing some of these norms, such as the idea that you should not consciously injure another person with your words. Artists are also able to take far more freedoms than most: they have a relatively high degree of autonomy in their work, and they are left at the end of it with a product that belongs to them, since they claim authorship over it. This represents a privilege—one that creative workers in start-ups, for example, can only dream of.

The oft-cited polarization of political conditions in our current climate can equally be applied to my own circle of friends, which has itself recently been dominated by the tendency toward factionalism, black-and-white thinking, and tribalist politics that know only friend and enemy. Even those who a short time ago would engage in lively and controversial debates are no longer prepared to share a word with one another. And yet there are also numerous historical precedents for this unforgiving behavior toward one's friends. Consider Albert Camus and Francis Ponge: their friendship fell apart because Camus could not bear his friend identifying as a communist; he subsequently distanced himself from Ponge, and their correspondence came to an end, as their letters attest. That Camus was unable to maintain an exchange with Ponge is symptomatic of the splits on the left that we encounter to this day: representatives of the radical left like Ponge have a hard time with left-wing liberals they deem to be insufficiently radical, too reformist, or too compromised, while left-wing liberals reject the totalizing abolitionist gestures of the radical left.

My own attempts to bring together those who until only recently cultivated a friendly exchange but have now fallen out for similar political reasons also failed. The fronts seem to have hardened, and everyone appears to be thoroughly entrenched in their respective positions; anyone who believes another to have taken the wrong political path now prefers not to enter any discussion with them at all. I do believe it would be a political mistake to enter into a dialogue with, for example, the much-invoked "intellectual right," since there is no shared frame of reference for such a discussion. But among progressive leftists and left-wing liberals, to have a conversation should be possible.

**9.6.2020**

With some of my male artist friends, it was their misogynistic behavior that forced me to break off contact with them—I could no longer bear their company. When we did encounter one another, they would find subtle ways of letting me know that, as a woman, I was not viewed as their equal. They were polite, at times even treating me with an exaggerated, obsequious humility, and yet it seemed a foregone conclusion that they would never refer to my work publicly. They mostly referenced their fellow male colleagues, and this happened especially when there was power or influence at stake. In such situations, you could bet your life they would only encourage and support their male buddies, since the guiding constellation of their shared universe was ultimately made up entirely of men.

It was only through others that I learned they found my theories, such as my ideas on the value of art, to be "touching." I realized that their condescending attitude toward me was, in psychoanalytic terms, a defense mechanism against the threat of the "phallic woman." But I eventually grew sick of having to empathize with their castration anxieties, especially since they were aggressively directed against me. I reduced my contact with these men to the minimum required for my work. Lo and behold, their behavior changed the moment they no longer represented a point of reference for me. This happened recently when I happened to run into a writer friend who had consistently ignored my books (while his novels, by contrast, were an importance reference for me in my younger years). Now, suddenly, he informed me how much he had enjoyed my last book. Perhaps my withdrawal from these oedipal relationships meant he could finally approach me as an author of equal status?

But to have reoriented (or even broken) myself away from men like this renowned writer, or from painters and fellow critics whom I consider significant, also carried certain risks. I feared they would try to undermine me, since I clearly no longer belonged to the ranks of their admirers. Given the increased importance ascribed to the approval of others since the postwar period, to refuse it can have fatal consequences. In his book *The Lonely Crowd*, the sociologist David Riesman postulates the emergence of an "other-directed character" within consumer society that increasingly orients itself around others and requires their validation. If these others—potential instances of legitimation—withdraw from a relationship, it would greatly threaten the other-directed character. Should they feel someone is denying them approval and recognition, they will punish them by placing obstacles in their path. My own sense of self, incidentally, also suffers when former friends turn away from me, since their validation gave me strength and held me together. To be oriented toward others ultimately also implies a greater dependency on our friends. For should they distance themselves from us and deny us the validation we crave, we are left weak, disoriented, and depleted.

**9.7.2020**

I lay awake last night thinking about why so many of my friendships have fallen apart in the last few months. Might it be connected to the enormous pressure we all face in this year of pandemic? The virus triggers fears and insecurities that are sometimes hard to bear; perhaps we can only deal with the tension this produces by offloading it and separating it from ourselves. Have I displaced the inner turmoil I feel due to the pandemic onto supposedly "bad" or "disappointing" friends, as a way of freeing myself from a pressure that had become unbearable? The ambivalent feelings that are natural within friendships are harder to integrate in a crisis such as this one. Life in lockdown is already stressful enough, and so we seek to free ourselves from anything that might represent an additional burden to us—complicated friendships, for example.

But I have also observed the opposite tendency: that people now nurture their friendships more than ever as a result of the pandemic. Certain friends whom I had not heard from for a long time now regularly check how I am, while contact with my close friends has also increased, since the absence of any social and cultural activities means we are all leading amputated lives. Despite all the differences in our personal circumstances, this crisis has also brought us together, and we now send each other tips for coping with everyday pandemic life—which films and online concerts are worth seeing, which yoga courses we find helpful, and so on.

So while this pandemic year has put an end to some of my friendships, others have intensified, and new friendly alliances have emerged. With more time to read, I have also discovered numerous authors—such as Ilse Aichinger, Jhumpa Lahiri, and Tine Rahel Völcker—whose nuanced and self-reflexive writing inspire me even in the face of the increasingly divisive climate the pandemic has produced. By contrast, I am no longer convinced by the self-assured and knowing pose I have observed in other authors. While political conflicts can force one to take a clear stance on an issue, anyone who believes themselves to be on the right side of the argument from the very beginning is ignoring the contradiction in their own position. In this pandemic, I feel more drawn to the tentative and cautious approach of thinkers who do not purport to have all the answers, such as Klaus Theweleit. Instead of issuing decrees, I think it's more appropriate to address the feelings the crisis brings up, like a lack of control and sense of disorientation. To abandon the posture of the sovereign and coherent subject does not have to mean pursuing a coquettish form of self-reflection, and I believe it is possible to admit doubt and uncertainty while still taking a clear position. In a situation such as this, I prefer to listen to those voices that underline the provisional and disputable nature of their own positions.

Now more than ever, it is the tone of a text that gives it its character for me, and I react almost allergically to self-assured tones and totalizing cultural analyses, preferring the tentative approach of provisional hypotheses and cautious inferences. Where I used to have something of an aversion to any appearance of an "I" in academic texts, the first-person narrative now strikes me as more suitable for capturing the existential impact of this crisis on our lives. To speculate about the situation in general often feels uncomfortably presumptuous; for an author to describe their place within this situation and to reveal the contingency of their own work seems far preferable to me.

**9.8.2020**

Since the first lockdown back in March, when all cultural institutions closed down, the freelancers in my circle of friends (self-employed actors, DJs, etc.) have had to battle massive existential fears. One complained to me that her more financially secure friends seemed incapable of showing any understanding for her situation; instead of empathizing with the worries and problems she faced, they would only emphasize the threat to their own lifestyles.

That the burdens of the pandemic are unevenly distributed is also ignored by some of my better-off friends, who seem more concerned with ensuring that their vacation plans are realized against all odds. One alternative would be to use the money to help friends less fortunate than themselves. Egocentrism and selfishness stand out more clearly than ever in the pandemic; it creates fissures within friendship groups and leads to new divisions. While my academic colleagues can enjoy the extra time gained through canceled talks and meetings by focusing on their writing, others (such as restaurant and boutique owners) are faced with ruin.

A further gulf has emerged between my friends with families. On the one side are those parents who, like me, are lucky enough that their children are receiving online lessons. Since I usually work from home anyway, and as my daughter currently attends school online between 9 a.m. and 4 p.m., I can work as normal. On the other side are the many parents who now have to stand in for their children's teachers themselves, as online lessons are not available. The fact that these parents must also work puts them under enormous pressure and brings them to the point of exhaustion.

It also makes a considerable difference if one weathers the pandemic alone or as part of a relationship or family. My single friends see themselves as being "punished" with loneliness by restrictions on face-to-face contact, while traditional living situations are, by contrast, rewarded, unless one has the misfortune of living in an unhappy marriage or dysfunctional family. For one friend, being stuck in close quarters with her family for so long led initially to arguments, and eventually to domestic violence. No longer able to work away from home, her husband first hit her, and then the children. Thankfully, my friend immediately informed the police and child services; her husband is no longer allowed to come near the children, and we—her friends—have formed a support network to help her.

Families and patchwork families like mine, by contrast, who live in relative harmony despite occasional conflicts, can enjoy family life during lockdown. While such differences in living situations could previously be glossed over between friends, they can have dramatic consequences in a pandemic, making them harder to bridge. Anyone who has been badly hit by the crisis does not want to be constantly reminded by their friends how much easier it is when one has a supportive partner or happy home; the pandemic thus serves to strengthen friendships between those of similar situations, while overcoming "differences" within a friendship (including different approaches to the crisis) is made more difficult. I currently have less to do with those friends who are determined to ensure their Caribbean vacation goes ahead at any cost, despite the lockdown. I am more connected to those who, like me, enjoy the relative privilege of sitting at their desks and trying to work, without the usual external pressures and incentives.

I too sometimes feel dejected by this crisis, and particularly by the loss of any public social life. Without outside stimulation from shared dinners with friends, or from closing discussions with colleagues at conferences, it's hard to discipline myself to push ahead with my writing projects, this one included. In a recent radio interview, the sociologist Harmut Rosa pointed out that contact with others generates energy in us. I do indeed currently lack the usual motivation for my projects. The loss of the energy I usually gain from exchanges with friends and colleagues has left me feeling permanently depleted. The lack of any immediate sounding board for my ideas means my current routine—of stubbornly writing away at home—can appear futile.

**9.9.2020**

In the first months of the pandemic, I observed how negative affects like jealousy and competitive behavior were running rampant within my circle of friends. This may have been because the cake we all shared had been significantly reduced, causing us to fight all the harder for the few remaining commissions and opportunities to make money. The willingness to trample on others in order to further one's own career seemed more strongly pronounced, and I have likely never experienced so little solidarity or even outright hostile behavior from some of my friends and colleagues. The pandemic possibly encourages us to act badly, since lockdown means there is no immediate prospect of bumping into those we have mistreated. That even so-called friends can end up attacking one another under these conditions can be seen on social media, where online bullying, trolling, and hate speech are more common than ever. There is equally little reason to fear running into our online friends "IRL" for the time being, and so there is essentially nothing stopping us from defaming them personally.

Beyond this, it is the structure of social media itself that is currently fueling our descent into the divisive logic of friends versus enemies. For it offers us just two possibilities: either we "like" the activities of our friends or we reject them—there is no place here for shades of meaning, nuance, or ambivalence. That the vehemently rejected position may not be entirely wrong but is, perhaps, partly worth considering is hard to communicate on Twitter or Facebook where our "friends" (by now entirely abstract) are either praised to the heavens or damned outright.

This reduction to "like" and "not like" makes me long for the *Streitkultur* (culture of debate) in 1970s German media. While far from perfect—one need only think of the dominance of sexist white men, usually with a cigarette in hand—it did at least allow for some productive disputes. To concede to one's opponent in certain points while rejecting others was both possible and entirely conceivable. Sites like Facebook deliberately exclude the possibility of gray areas, since unlike likes, complex comments do not function as a quantifiable currency (of appreciation and depreciation), while the purely abstract nature of our online friends also makes it easier to give in to the impulse for division. Social media therefore seems to be dangerous ground for friendships. A misplaced or missing like can cause sustained resentments among online friends; I have even heard of friendships collapsing for this reason, since an absence of likes is now often read as marking their end.

**9.10.2020**

The fact that the entire world currently seems to be spending its time on social media means that I am reminded of the benefits of the physical presence of another. Were online haters to stand directly in front of the people they bully, they might realize they actually quite like them. It is also easier to clear up the misunderstandings that arise during online disputes in direct conversation. In this time of absent friends (and enemies), I realize more than ever that they are each in some way a part of me—that I carry them with me, as it were.

Derrida addresses this theme of absent-present friends in *The Politics of Friendship*, with an interesting reference to Heidegger's description of a "Dasein" (being there) that "carries" a friend with it. As stimulating as Derrida's book is, I must admit that I silently groan whenever I come across exclusively male (and often politically dubious) thinkers like Heidegger, Carl Schmitt, or Nietzsche in its pages. But for all my skepticism toward Heidegger, I nonetheless find his concept of Dasein thought-provoking in the context of friendship. For him, this Dasein is one in which the friend (who, again, is exclusively conceived as male) is fundamentally embedded; the friend serves as its ground and is thus inherent to it. Our current Dasein under the conditions of a pandemic would likely appear incomplete and amputated to Heidegger, since our friends are absent. After all, at the start of the first lockdown in March, we were told that it is a sign of friendship to avoid contact with our friends—that is, to banish them from our lives/Dasein. This makes me wonder if we really do have to see our friends for them to enter our Dasein, or if they remain a part of it even when absent.

While Aristotle considered the immediate presence of a friend to be the precondition of friendship, this postulate of proximity gets underminded in a pandemic by the imperative that we avoid contact with others. I find his notion of a friendship based on physical presence to be hopelessly outdated in any case, since it does not consider friendships conducted via media (above all those of written correspondence such as letters, or later WhatsApp messages, which naturally did not exist in Aristotle's time). Under the conditions of a lockdown, one might argue (in line with Derrida and against Aristotle) for a deconstructive understanding of friendship that places absence and distance front and center. But this would merely swap one extreme for the other: instead of presence, it is absence that is now declared to be the prerequisite of friendship.

In fact, there are numerous friendships that—as if imagined by Derrida—get by without the physical presence of the friend, as with long-distance relationships (made significantly harder in a pandemic by the difficulties in traveling). But the weeks of lockdown also demonstrated the enormous merits of the physical company of friends, whose presence was painfully missed everywhere. It therefore seems as if Aristotle's concept of friendship currently applies more than Derrida's: friendship does require a physical presence. Should this be impossible, we long for it all the more. For me, an eloquent image of this longing was provided by those friends who regularly met for walks in the Tiergarten during the lockdown, regardless of the weather, since the restrictions imposed on personal contact meant this was the only opportunity for them to see one another. I, too, was willing to put up with the discomfort of trudging along in the cold, since it allowed me to be physically close to my friends; walking alongside each other meant we were able to directly engage with one another. I had several such walks with various friends during lockdown, and I returned home each time feeling happy and fulfilled.

**9.11.2020**

Like everyone else, I have spent more time than ever at home during this pandemic. (By "everyone else," I mean everyone who has a home; I also exclude those often invoked essential workers who, like hospital staff, are required to work long hours away from theirs.) The fact that many of my professional responsibilities have fallen away means I should have more free time than ever, which I resolved to use productively for my writing. This put me under enormous pressure. Each morning I would compulsively check the latest corona news, and I then had to overcome the anxieties caused by the rising infection and death rates before I could really get going.

My writing got off to a slow start. The mere thought of the countless people suffering and dying in intensive care wards was enough to take my breath away, and I wondered what sense there could be in writing a book on friendship under such conditions. But I also knew from my experience of earlier (personal) crises that my only option in such a situation was to stay resolutely focused on my work. The daily ritual of writing brings a degree of structure to a life that has spun out of control—like a life preserver, it keeps me afloat. At some point, the text draws me into its own logic and allows me to block out the depressing reality of the world outside for a moment. As debilitating as this pandemic is, it also pushes me. For if every breath or encounter is potentially fatal, I should ensure that my "body of work" is in order beforehand. So I continue to work on this book, as if I might somehow outwit the virus through my writing.

The pandemic's existential dimension has also forced me to take a closer look at my personal and family situation. Do I really want to live like this? Which of my relationships are still coherent in the face of the crisis? It was therefore fitting to read in the press that many relationships and marriages fell apart during the first lockdown. The constant physical proximity this imposed on those living together meant that many couples could no longer hide their aversion to one another—they had to separate. One friend of mine, a lawyer specializing in family law, told me of the recent increase in petitions for divorce. People would start by cleaning out their basements and closets, she said, before going on to test the state of their marriages (and relationships).

While I was gripped by a similar determination to "take inventory" of my life, this did not relate to my family, whom I spent many happy hours with during lockdown. Instead, it was my relationships with friends that needed closer scrutiny. I realized that I had hung on to some for far too long, despite the humiliations and pain they regularly inflicted upon me. And yet I had also contributed to the destructive dynamic of these friendships. I ran through the situations where I might have offended the people in question (whether willingly or unwillingly), and I reproached myself for having clung on to these unhealthy friendships out of an unreflective sense of emotional attachment. That I continued these relationships for so long may also have been because they positioned my work within a social context I was reluctant to fall out of. From the isolation of lockdown life, I contemplated various scenarios: I could simply let them taper off, silently withdrawing myself, or I could do it "officially," clarifying things with a final conversation.

The latter of these options—to end a friendship with a discussion—would take courage, as I knew from my earlier attempts at talking openly to Peter, my long-time artist friend. There were several occasions where I tried to tell him that his behavior sometimes caused me pain, and that I found certain of his comments to be hurtful. Peter generally reacts adversely to such disclosures. If I articulate my feelings, he can become downright hostile; it might be that the mere fact of me opening up to him is enough to trigger his anxieties and defense mechanisms. Is it because of these anxieties that he becomes aggressive with me whenever I address the problems I feel exist within our friendship? Or is it simply that I can't find the right words myself? Is it my fault that we are unable to talk to one another?

In part, I also fear another "moment of truth" since, for a long time, we've had an unspoken pact: our friendship itself, or our possible feelings of irritation or disappointment with each other, was never to be made a topic of direct conversation, even if we always discussed everything else at length.

I greatly valued these conversations with Peter, particularly appreciating his sharp analytic insight into the power relations and consensus-building processes of the art world. Discussing its current events and developments with him was hugely inspiring, amusing, and enjoyable for me. But we also tended to push things that were simmering between us—the disappointments and irritations we felt toward one another—under the carpet. We could happily discuss anything except our relationship. And over time, this muzzle we had silently imposed on each other became hard for me to live with.

I am reluctant to break things off with Peter. In doing so, I would be following the dictum that we should instantly abandon anyone who is not "good for us"—a tenet of self-help culture that I have always loathed. This idea struck me as dubious from the start, since declaring "mutual affirmation" to be the defining characteristic of friendship means it is once again defined in terms of its benefits. Should it no longer provide us with these benefits, it is no longer useful and must be ended. I do not want to treat my own friendships in such an instrumental and selfish way, especially since, for one thing, there were numerous situations in which Peter's company did benefit me. For another, I often value him for the fact that he has not made me feel good, that he has challenged or confronted me with uncomfortable truths. But the maxim of affirmative friendships excludes the idea that they can include a negative or destructive element. A friendship must be purely good or else it is bad and must be discarded. In this context, do I simply need to learn to be more tolerant of ambiguity, and to continue my friendship with Peter despite all its difficulties? Or has a line been crossed when I leave an encounter with him feeling humiliated and disheartened? I am not ready to declare this friendship dead, even if it sometimes torments me.

**9.12.2020**

I have already noted that the pandemic means many people are currently sitting at home and spending more time on social media. A positive view of social media platforms is that they create connections and help lend a voice to marginalized groups, such as ethnic minorities or the LGBTQ+ community. With the #MeToo movement, it was on Facebook and Twitter that victims of sexual violence were finally able to be heard. At the same time, our willingness to attack and defame others (including our "friends") also rises within this sphere, since it is easy to block out the devastating psychological effects that hate posts have on the people targeted.

I myself am only too familiar with this. I have become a target of cyberbullying in recent years, whether it is someone posting images of me as a corpse on Instagram or an attempt to discredit me by quoting passages of an interview out of context. The creator of the corpse images was likely living out a destructive fantasy—a need to see the "overly powerful" woman killed and eradicated. The Facebook friend who posted the shortened quote probably had something else in mind: he wanted to delegitimize my work. Of course, there can be a concrete reason for such posts, when my behavior or something I say is badly received. But the drastic way such criticisms are leveled at me demonstrates that it's not merely a case of arguing with my work, but of damaging me as a person. Or perhaps the reverse is true: my work is viewed critically (with good reason), but social media provides no suitable space for this critical engagement. There, criticism usually tips over into personal defamation.

According to my therapist, envy (again) can sometimes serve as fertile ground for these hate posts. The texts of Melanie Klein are instructive in this respect: envy, she claims, ultimately articulates a destructive desire that is directed against the creative energy of the envied person, which must be destroyed. That the posts in question were intended to silence me and rob me of my vigor was clear from the way in which they exhausted me not just physically but mentally. Each time I discovered one of them I felt thunderstruck—numb, weakened, and dejected. To pull myself out of the depression it triggered and regain my strength took an unbelievable amount of effort, and I repeatedly told myself I wouldn't let the screeching of these (mostly male) trolls rob me of my energy and optimism. Easier said than done.

**9.13.2020**

I recently read the letters exchanged between Hannah Arendt and Mary McCarthy in the 1950s and 1960s. They were best friends and both writers—Arendt a philosopher, McCarthy a novelist. For me, their correspondence serves as touching proof that the model friendships of the twentieth century were to be found less among men (contrary to what Derrida believed) and more among women (or those who identify as women). At the same time, friendship between women is often characterized by a high degree of care—that is, by behavior traditionally connoted as "feminine." According to Janosch Schobin, female friendships, such as that between Arendt and McCarthy, have now become a model for friendship in general. Friendships today have to be caring, he claims, otherwise they would be unworthy of the label friendship.

The norm of caring friendship that Schobin observes may now be prevalent in society. Within my own milieu of the art world, however, friendships based on care are the exception; there, it is friendship as a form of cooperation aimed at benefiting those involved that predominates. It should be acknowledged that friendly care and utility-oriented cooperation can merge at times, as with Arendt and McCarthy's correspondence. Not only did both women support each other in their personal lives, navigating one another through difficult situations and offering help when needed, but they also regularly stood up for each other's work in public. Should one of them come under heavy attack, as Arendt did for her book on Eichmann, the other would not delay in publishing a statement of support for her friend. This worked both ways: when McCarthy found herself confronted with sexist insults from Norman Mailer after publishing *The Group*, Arendt immediately put pen to paper in defense of the literary value of McCarthy's novel.

Naturally, I ask myself if my close friends and colleagues would jump into the breach for me in a similar situation. This strikes me as unlikely. Arendt and McCarthy's mutual engagement was surely made easier by the fact that there was no immediate element of competition within their relationship: they were active in different fields, meaning neither of them got in the way of the other's career. And yet I would not expect to receive any comparable form of public support from my friends, even those outside my professional context.

I recently conducted a mini survey among my author colleagues on the question of whether friends can be expected to provide public backing in situations of personal attack. The result: no one would hope for any such support. Should one's book be unfairly torn apart, the most that might be expected is for some consolation and encouragement to be offered on the personal level. What was taken for granted by Arendt and McCarthy—that friends would speak out for each other publicly—seems to be unthinkable in the framework of today's friendships.

I wonder what the reason for this could be. Why did it not occur to any of my friends to defend me during the most recent round of cyberbullying attacks, or at least to put the (mostly male) perpetrators in their place? Perhaps it's because such attacks are so common these days. In explaining their reluctance to speak out, they tell me they feared that defending me on social media would simply add fuel to the fire and ultimately inflict more damage. This suspicion is probably correct, but it does nothing to change my longing for support—my hope that someone will leap to my side and (publicly) defend me. I should admit, however, that I myself do not always necessarily offer others the support I crave.

It seems to me as if this reticence also has a deeper cause. Not only are my friends and colleagues often my collaborators, but we also sometimes compete with one another. Should cooperation and competition merge, as in Kai van Eikels's concept of cocompetition, this can in extreme cases cause my collaborator to mutate into my rival, and maybe even my enemy—or frenemy. If most of our cooperative relationships become permeated with competition, this might reduce our willingness to fend off damage to a colleague's reputation by, for instance, publicly supporting her work. For in structural terms, one has a far greater interest (mostly unconscious, naturally) in this competitor falling behind in her career as a result of these attacks, and in the worst case even suffering substantial damage to her reputation. This, too, may partly explain our reluctance to intervene when one of us is harassed online. Structural conditions push us to behavior that does not meet my demands for ethical action. To endure this tension between self-interest and the ideal of unselfish friendship is particularly hard for me these days, when I long for intimate friendship.

**9.14.2020**

For several months now, it has seemed as if Peter is turning his back on me, treating me and my work with increasing indifference. When I inform him of the current state of a text, he listens with one ear, and he never asks about my projects, as if seeking to signal his disinterest in them. A photo recently fell into my hands that shows the two of us in a public discussion, me speaking and him listening. The expression with which he's reacting to my remarks speaks volumes: it appears dismissive, if not downright hostile. Or am I just imagining it all—could my perception of this photograph be exaggerated by my underlying doubts regarding his loyalty? My sensitivity has taken on unimaginable proportions since entering menopause; my once thick skin is gone, and I am highly receptive to aggressions and negative feelings around me. It is therefore possible that I am exaggerating the intensity of Peter's rejection. Maybe he is just a weirdo who acts strangely from time to time. Nonetheless, the photo seems to me to speak a clear message. While Peter said nothing that might have suggested an aversion to me, his body language in this photo suggests he has fundamental misgivings about me and my work. Or does he secretly even hate me a little?

That my relationship to Peter still falls under the label of "friendship" is something I myself must answer for. For years on end, I sought and initiated exchanges and meetings with him. There were times when we were emotionally close and coached each other through crises in our love affairs and personal lives. Peter wrote me long emails of encouragement when I experienced the pain of separation, and I, too, supported him in lengthy phone calls when his relationship of many years fell apart. Peter did not allow me to be subsumed in heartache; in his view, it was essential that my work be the highest priority. He encouraged me not to make my well-being dependent on my love life; for him, it was the work alone that counted.

Correspondingly, the focus of our friendship was on "professional matters," meaning our encounters frequently had the character of work sessions, where issues regarding our careers were worked through. This often involved tactical advice: Should we accept certain invitations, and what strategies should we pursue in dealing with the indignities and violations that befell us in the artistic field? Peter also bolstered my spirits when the many acts of sexist discrimination I experienced left me feeling worn out and fragile.

In retrospect, however, it seems my commitment to his career was greater and my support for his work more unconditional than his engagement with my own affairs. He would likely see this differently. What is certain, though, is that we have now reached a stage where we no longer require the other's support so urgently. That is not to say that our careers are totally secure—as we all know, no one can rest on their laurels since the onset of late modernity, with each of us required to constantly prove ourselves anew. But Peter and I are by now both established enough that our battle for attention and recognition has lost some of its intensity.

It is therefore no coincidence that our friendship is being put to the test now of all times. Peter has experienced a degree of institutional recognition for his sculptures that makes my assistance superfluous. If I really think about it, I have always supported his artistic production, while he has often responded to my texts with a dry skepticism, as if underlining their deficiencies. By contrast, he always showed the cultural output of our male colleagues (whether photographers, painters, or writers) a far higher degree of respect, considering anything these men produced to be inherently meaningful—unlike my texts, where there was always some fault to be found. He seemed to take it for granted that my own works would never reach the level of the texts written by my male counterparts. In retrospect, I am amazed that Peter regularly devaluing my work (even if unintentionally) didn't cause me to give it up. Only in rare cases did he offer concrete praise. But the opposite was actually the case: instead of discouraging me, his criticism and deprecation spurred me on to make the next text better, to work harder and ensure it was more finely honed. That Peter never really believed in me (or didn't seem to) was to some extent a perverse gift: it was the absence of his approval that drove me to continue, and I made ever greater efforts to convince him of my worth. His lack of respect for my work was also an expression of an unspoken hierarchy, at the top of which stood, in his eyes, visual art. While writing about it was essential, it was also of a fundamentally secondary nature.

But the older I got, the harder I found it to cope with the destructive nature of this friendship pact. Each meeting with Peter left me feeling dejected, with my writing blocked for days as a result of his refusal to acknowledge it. Luckily, I had by then developed friendships with other colleagues from whom I received more support for my work. While it was increasingly difficult to bear the corrosive effects Peter's behavior had on my self-esteem, I also found out how much better I could work when I was being supported by sympathetic friends.

At some point, I made the decision to confront Peter with my feelings, and to make it clear that his lack of interest in my work offended me. But this attempt at baring my injured soul to him backfired. His voice sharp, he instantly accused me of overreacting, claiming I was only ever interested in myself. No word of apology, no "I'm sorry I hurt your feelings." That his reaction was so defensive and aggressive shocked me, but it also made me realize the hopelessness of this friendship. While I may not yet be ready to withdraw from it for good, it has already taken the first step toward its dissolution.

What holds me back from ending it is our deep connection. We often understand each other without the need for words—the mere expression on the other's face is enough to let us know what they think about something. Peter is never taken in by what everyone else thinks; in the battle against hastily drawn conclusions, he is my ally. Should I have misgivings about a phenomenon that is praised by all, I can assume he will have similar reservations. The fact that we are bound together by decades of shared survival within the art milieu also makes me reluctant to sever this bond; Peter and I share a history that I do not want to deny or dismiss. The many conversations I have had with him have made me who I am. Simone de Beauvoir writes somewhere that we would not be ourselves without others, and this is equally true of me: without my exchanges with Peter, my self would be a different one.

If I reflect upon our friendship more closely, I must admit that I was always aware of its potential for failure. After all, as intimate attachments, friendships are inherently precarious structures. In the case of my friendship with Peter, I have for years now accepted that he would turn his back on me the moment I fell into disfavor or no longer exhibited any signs of success. And that is precisely what did happen. After the aforementioned talk provoked controversy and brought me into disrepute within a certain section of the art world, he seemed to distance himself from me. It was as if the wind turning against me had caused him to join the ranks of my critics. In our subsequent meetings, he would find subtle ways of letting me know that my opinion now counted for less. He showed a certain indifference toward my words, as if they had lost their validity; in his eyes, I had suffered a significant blow to my authority.

What keeps me bound to him despite this is an unspoken agreement between us. For years, I (willingly) played the role of the "stronger" friend who stood by his side, while he took the position of the weaker counterpart who needed my support and backing. Perhaps I allocated him this "weaker" role so that I could be in control. This unhealthy dynamic found its expression in the ritual that played out at the end of our meetings in cafés. I always felt compelled to pay the check, even though he had long earned more than I did; since my role was that of the better-off friend, I reflexively reached for my wallet. I might have been symbolically acting out my role as the one who must "pay" for this friendship. Moreover, since I am presumed to be the "stronger" party in our relationship, with a supposedly more secure position, Peter can expect me to accept his harsh criticism of my work. It is precisely because I am (apparently) so firmly established that I have to endure this criticism. Each encounter with him is tantamount to a test of my self-esteem: How much humiliation can it bear, and at what point does it collapse?

Writing these thoughts by hand, I realize that my dissatisfaction at the dynamic of my friendship with Peter is growing deeper. Perhaps this is causing me to give an overly one-sided account of our relationship; anyone reading these words may wonder if my support of his work was really as unconditional as I have portrayed it. I have to admit that my backing was itself a double-edged sword. For it may have been based on an unconscious desire that he remain unsuccessful in spite of it. Had institutional recognition and commercial success evaded him, this would have increased his dependency on me. He would have been reliant on my support, which I likely unconsciously longed for. I wanted to look after him, and still do, but my help is no longer needed. His great institutional and commercial success has made me redundant. In any case, this was what Peter communicated in his last emails to me. He offered no response to my accounts of my own work, while speaking obsessively about himself—or, more accurately, his work, which seemed to be the only thing that counted. My only remaining function was as an addressee for his monologue, now easily replaceable.

Peter's view of the situation is surely a different one, and he likely sees me as guilty of the same self-centeredness I find so difficult to bear in him. I can imagine him finding my portrayal of his behavior to be narcissistic and maudlin—narcissistic because I place myself at the center of everything, and maudlin because I underestimate both my own position of power as a critic and the respect he shows my texts. Instead, I self-pityingly gripe about a situation that, in his view, in no way justifies such an account. And in a way, he is right: my complaints are undeniably those of a fortunate person. But this does not make them entirely groundless, and I still want to be heard by him, in spite of everything.

**9.15.2020**

I had a strong sense this morning of just how worrying and distressing my unresolved friendship situation with Peter has become for me. Of course, it's not his fault that I've changed in recent years and now expect more from myself and my friends, such as consistently compassionate, empathetic, and caring behavior. My last meeting with him was a fiasco in this respect. After I had extensively viewed his latest works—a series of minimalistic objects with painterly finishes on their outer surfaces—he mentioned that my last book, *The Voice of the Others*, is in his eyes "not literature," and that it also contains two spelling mistakes. It was never my intention to make any claim to "great literature" with this auto-fictional project. But to locate my text outside of the literary world from the very beginning seemed to amount to a denial of its very right to existence. How would Peter have reacted if I had described his works as nonart and pointed out a flaw in their paintwork? As he well knows, I took a great risk in writing my book. In it, I opened myself up for the first time, dealing with personal issues like the grief I felt upon losing my parents. Why was he so unwilling to value my attempt to find a language for talking about powerful emotions like rage and disappointment? Unfortunately, I am rarely able to formulate a suitable response to such indignities in the moment, and so it was in this case, too: I felt paralyzed, and I wanted nothing but to urgently flee and free myself from this painful situation. Abruptly, I stood up and said goodbye, practically running out of his studio.

It was only the next day that I realized how much Peter's comment had hurt me, as I sat before my laptop in a state of creative and spiritual crisis. My ideas for new books now seemed presumptuous and futile, doomed to failure from the start. Lacking any drive, I simply sat there, staring gloomily at the keyboard. The only relief came from my resolution that I would no longer submit myself to Peter's hurtful remarks in the future; I would end our friendship and never again set foot in his studio.

That our meeting had gone badly and left me upset seemed to have passed him by entirely. The tone of his subsequent emails was the same as ever, as if he expected I would simply reappear at his studio in a few weeks. Reading his words, a feeling of outrage grew within me. I had an urgent need to finally speak my mind, to call him up and shout at him without restraint. But I also knew from experience that to respond in such an emotional way would get us nowhere; while it creates a feeling of relief, it ultimately does nothing to alter the problematic logic of the relationship. I considered letting the friendship run out instead, but ghosting isn't my style. And since we were sure to continue encountering one another in social situations in the future, I felt I should clarify things between us.

While I considered expressing my anger to him in writing, I decided this would also be the wrong path to take. I didn't want him to have something on paper that might one day become public following our deaths, since his newfound prominence meant there was likely to be a posthumous interest in his correspondence. The more I struggled with the question of what approach to take, the more the positive aspects of our friendship forced their way into my thoughts. We had always enjoyed an inspiring exchange of ideas, for example, complementing each other perfectly in our thoughts on art, such as when visiting exhibitions together. We would also often analyze the various micro-dramas within our circle of friends and colleagues. And so I anxiously asked myself if I could afford to forgo these valuable shared microanalyses. Did I not rely on Peter's original perspective on these matters, and might my own thinking and writing suffer without his input?

In order not to abandon those aspects of our friendship that did function well, I had attempted several months previously to transform it into a purely professional alignment. This model had proven to be impracticable, since I had repeatedly fallen into old patterns of behavior when communicating with him, trusting him with personal information that wouldn't have concerned him if he were just my colleague. I would instinctively tell him about problems I was experiencing with my teenage daughter, or of the disappointment I felt at the behavior of certain mutual friends. Out of habit, I had slipped into a mode of intimacy with him that had not been appropriate to our relationship for some time. My behavior was practically compulsive, and I was clearly not in any position to establish a distanced form of communication with him.

**9.16.2020**

I have now succeeded in removing myself from this painful alliance. It wasn't nearly as bad as I feared. I told Peter up-front that I wanted to end the friendship, before asking him if he wished to know the reasons. He was visibly shocked by my sudden announcement, but he appeared to be interested in my explanation. I told him how hurt I had been by his comment regarding my book, and by what I felt to be his generally disinterested attitude toward my work. He seemed stunned and assured me that this wasn't the case. I realized that the hostility I had felt had not been perceived as such by him. Could the idea that he didn't respect me just have been a projection on my part, I wondered? And yet it was also telling that he did not fight to save our friendship; on the contrary, he calmly agreed to the separation, accepting it, though not without regret. I reassured him that it was not his fault, that my expectations of friendship had simply changed, and I expressed my hope that we could maintain a productive exchange as colleagues in the future.

Above all, I was tired of my own behavior in our relationship. Against my better judgment, I had repeatedly fallen into the logic of the transactional friendship in my dealings with Peter, feeding him insider knowledge or suggestions that I didn't actually want to pass on to him. It was depressing to see how reflexively I acted out my part. His lack of interest in my work also seemed to have become more rigid. Might he have unconsciously looked down on me for not having ended the friendship sooner?

Beyond this, I also feel a growing resistance to my role as a service provider. Critics have the power to produce meaning, formulate judgments, and initiate reappraisals—work that means a great deal to me. And yet I am increasingly reluctant to garland the work of radically self-centered artists by providing them with catalogue texts. That art criticism now stands among the bottom rungs of the art business is also something I've registered with unease. This hierarchy did not always exist; even until the 1980s, critics and theorists enjoyed influence and respect as figures of authority within their field. It was only recently, during the thirtieth-anniversary celebration of a Berlin gallery, that I realized a change had occurred in this regard. After the gallerist hosted a glamorous dinner for three hundred people, he addressed the attendees with a thank-you speech. He began by thanking all the artists present, followed by the collectors and curators, then finally (tellingly in last place) his wife. Critics, others of whom sat at the table alongside me, were not mentioned at all, as if they played absolutely no role in the art world's processes of value formation—as if they were a *quantité négligeable*. Later that evening, I gathered the courage to ask the gallerist if there was anyone he had forgotten in his speech. He didn't know whom I was referring to—the fact that he had ignored us critics hadn't even occurred to him.

It is also frequently the case that certain artist friends will find ways of letting me know that they are essentially number one, while my function is merely to interpret and communicate their concerns. Here it should be remembered that critics—and above all male critics—once enjoyed greater influence and significance within the art establishment. One thinks, for example, of the admiration shown by visual artists toward their writer and critic friends in the first half of the twentieth century, as with Jean Fautrier's friendships with Francis Ponge and Jean Paulhan. But a structural transformation that occurred within the art market in the 1990s means that symbolic value—and this applies above all to the commercial segment of the art industry—now counts for less than market success. And since the potential market success of a book cannot match that of a unique artwork, the image of writers and critics within this sphere is diminished: their symbolic capital is worth less than the money of the commercially successful.

The fact that Peter did not welcome my literary project may also be due to another reason. Critics are generally frowned upon when they abandon their usual terrain in order to write a novel—as with Susan Sontag, for example. (Although the negative reactions to Sontag's novels may also come down to the books themselves; I myself prefer her essays on cultural theory.) There is also the tacit expectation that critics continue to offer criticism and remain in the service of art at all times. Should they decide to take a more autonomous path in their work, the initial reaction is often one of skepticism. Beyond this, in creating their own personal works, they run the risk of exposing themselves as fallible, thus potentially devaluing their critical judgment.

It is therefore not only in the interest of artists that I remain in my usual place, but also in that of my own authority as a critic. It seems to me—though I might be imagining this—that many of my art-world friends would likely take an unsympathetic view were I to attempt to redefine myself; they would prefer I remain pigeonholed in the role they have allocated to me. My true friends, by contrast, support me in my efforts to broaden my radius of activities and break into new fields, even if they also point out the risks involved.

**9.17.2020**

The pandemic requires new borders to be drawn within friendships regarding what constitutes appropriate behavior. Anyone who insists on meeting others outdoors while infection rates are rising will have difficulties with those friends who continue to meet indoors and socialize in large groups, likely avoiding them where possible. Yesterday, I spoke to a friend on the phone who cheerily told me of the various invitations she had accepted in recent days, among them a dinner and even a reception. This stung me in two respects. On the one hand, I felt left out, since I currently receive almost no such invitations; my social life is largely fallow, and it feels as if barely anything happens at all if I don't take the initiative to arrange a walk or phone call myself. On the other hand, it strikes me as strange that while I rigidly stick to the rules and see no one outside of shared walks, some of my friends continue partying. One might get the impression that—as is so often the case within capitalism—it is those who flout the rules that are rewarded, while anyone who dutifully follows them loses out. I felt a similar sting when a collector friend of mine recently informed me that she would soon be escaping with her children to Gran Canaria; they can continue their online lessons there, she said. She asked me to keep this information to herself, since she planned to just take a rapid test and skip quarantine when they returned.

Anyone who escapes the bleak reality of Berlin under corona by going on vacation (or has access to a second home somewhere), as many well-off collectors have done, knowingly risks being stranded in a place with inadequate health care. At the same time, they are able to escape the monotonous and depressing reality of urban pandemic life and the rapidly rising infection rates of the big cities. And so, while less well-heeled artists and critics are stuck in their apartments, their movements limited to a few predictable circuits of their usual route, like a dog on a chain, the rich members of the art establishment have happily absconded to islands or mountain resorts, leaving the whole mess behind. They will return refreshed, skirting the regulations, while those of us who remained have to battle exhaustion and depression. It seems as if class relations are repeating themselves in a new way in the pandemic: the much-invoked one percent seems to be cultivating an attitude of "what matters most is that I'm alright," in which solidarity plays no role. In the face of such reckless behavior, I have to be careful not to become bitter toward my better-off acquaintances, furious at those who continue to enjoy their wealth while society suffers one crisis after another.

**9.18.2020**

That the global pandemic and its lockdowns present a stress test for friendships is also due to the fact that we currently feel called upon to avoid our friends as much as possible. I recently happened to bump into my friend Berenice during a walk; each of us stayed on our own side of the street, cautiously waving to each other from a distance.

From our mutual body language ("Stay back!"), it was clear that we each considered a closer physical encounter (even in the form of simply crossing the street and approaching one another) to be out of the question. Instead, we shouted a few words of greeting to one another before going our separate ways. The only purpose of this encounter was to avoid each other. I found it tragic that we, as friends, were so determined to give each other a wide berth despite our great mutual affection. The virus has created a gulf between us, like the "deep water" that keeps the king's children apart from one another in the German fairy tale. Except that the virus, unlike the water, is an invisible barrier.

And yet I also noticed around the end of the first lockdown in May that I could get along very well without in-person social interaction. I had to drag myself to the few appointments I did keep. What had once come easily to me—meetings with friends in restaurants and cafés—now cost me a great deal of effort. I was no longer used to such encounters, and I could sense the toll they took on my energy level. I found being at home for days on end to be restorative, if also depressing in the long term. The more I retreated into my private life, the more I had to make a conscious effort to ensure I even saw others. I sank into my own rhythm, moving between study and bedroom, kitchen and bathroom. Squeezed into this corset, I could make myself believe that I still hadn't completely lost control over my life.

**9.20.2020**

My feelings regarding my more problematic friendships also mellowed during the first lockdown, which I like everyone else spent in front of my computer screen. The resentment I had been harboring against some of my friends (such as Peter) vanished as if by magic. Instead, I felt drawn to them, which must have been an effect of the universal dimension of the virus: despite our differences, it forces its reality upon us all. Of course, it makes a considerable difference whether one spends quarantine in a house with a garden, in a tiny apartment with small children, or without a roof over one's head. But since most of my friends tend to come from middle-class backgrounds and often live—especially if they are older—in spacious old Berlin apartments, our situations during lockdown were comparable. From Zoom conferences (particularly endless for the teachers among us) to the forced reevaluation of others as potential risks, we all struggled with the same challenges. Each of us faced similar psychological issues as a result of the virus (anxiety, sleeplessness), and earlier differences of opinion appeared less significant when cast in this new light. I often felt a need to get in touch with precisely those friends with whom I had previously experienced some sort of upset, whether mild or severe; faced with a global crisis that had transformed our lives, these differences no longer played such an important role. I also checked in with friends who are single or live alone who often battle feelings of loneliness in the pandemic, or with those I knew to be trapped in broken marriages. During these many phone calls we would often compare notes, offering each other useful tips for dealing with this exceptional situation and telling each other of our new rituals, such as daily walks or online concerts—compensation for the endless hours we now spent sitting in front of our screens.

While most of my friends have been largely spared from the devastating psychological and economic effects of this pandemic, there is almost no one among them who has not experienced the situation as an enormous burden. We discussed our symptoms, such as increased irritability and muscle tension. Many of us reported grinding our teeth at night because of stress, resolving (as I did) to remedy this with a night guard. To me, these mouth guards seem to unite the outer pressure we feel in the pandemic with its attritional effect within us: we do not want to subject our teeth (and bodies) to the mental strain we feel in this crisis, which manifests itself in us unconsciously clenching our jaws. At the same time, we want to ensure our teeth remain intact and presentable, and are not worn down by grinding. The night guard is therefore emblematic of a dual pressure within this pandemic: that which comes from outside, and that which we put upon ourselves. We require instruments such as these in order to soote the internal pressure we feel while simultaneously yielding to external pressure. A peaceful night's sleep without such aids is almost unthinkable now. I draw upon an arsenal of soporific resources, among them a sleep mask and—paradoxically in this quiet time—earplugs, which my friends report they now also keep in their nightstands.

**9.22.2020**

According to Hannah Arendt, it is not only in times of misfortune that friendship is tested; it must also be capable of withstanding good fortune. I have experienced how this can indeed represent a touchstone for a friendship. Some of my friends have reacted with outright aggression when I enjoyed longer runs of good luck—the greater the opportunities and successes that came my way, the more distant and even hostile their behavior toward me became. Here, I recall 2018 with some horror—on the face of it, the year of my "success." In addition to finally passing my driving test (following some delay due to my fear of driving), I was awarded a prestigious grant that released me from teaching to work on a research project, and I also curated a commercial art exhibition in a gallery—a group show. By the end of that year, however, a close friend of mine—Paula—had cut ties between us, while other friends had also distanced themselves from me. Paula justified ending our friendship by expressing her incomprehension at my recent "life choices." She claimed that her primary concern was with the fact that I earned money from the exhibition I curated—for the first time in my life, incidentally. Other friends and acquaintances also resented me for muddying the critical ethos with economic interests. Their primary objection was that, by taking a financial interest in the works sold, I had forfeited my "freedom" as a critic. It was as if I had never been involved in compromising relationships of economic dependency beforehand—such as selling editions produced for the journal I founded. After all, these editions can themselves be understood as a program that demonstrates the entangled relationship that exists between art, criticism, and the market.

In the face of the increasing overlap between the commercial and critical spheres, I see it as the task of criticism to reflect upon its altered situation. It was not only for this reason that I was open about the financial arrangement between me and the gallery: I received a small commission from the sold works. By making no secret about this arrangement, I also wanted to point to the notoriously low fees critics receive in comparison to some of the artists they write about and also in comparison to the artists' gallerists, who often make big money.

It seemed to offend Paula that my financial situation improved as a result of the sales. She often struggles with money herself and informed me that, in her eyes, I had betrayed her, that I had sold my soul. In no way did I consider myself less free as a result of the exhibition, however; as I saw it, the fact that I had profited from the artworks on display did not stop me from viewing them critically. And yet I understood it was not easy for Paula to see that I could now afford a few luxury items that she herself—as I knew—also longed for. If the gap between friends' financial situations widens, it can put a strain on their relationship. For by adopting a more lavish lifestyle, the better-off friend shows the other what they are missing out on.

Paula made an attempt at asking me for money, but she is also known for rarely paying people back. I had learned from my therapy sessions that for one party to be indebted to the other for any sustained period can often be fatal for their relationship. I therefore decided against giving her the money, promising her other forms of support instead. My refusal seemed to be the last straw. She sent me a text announcing the end of our friendship, adding that its failure was entirely my own fault. For weeks I suffered feelings of guilt and regret at losing my friend. I had become so close to her in previous years that I often described her as an extra family member. Following our separation I occasionally stalked Paula on Instagram to find out what she was up to, and in this way feel closer to her.

Another reader of these pages asked me if I really want to allocate so much space to the acute conflicts in my friendships; in doing so, she claimed, I run the risk of lending them too much weight. This risk cannot be dismissed out of hand. But the truth is that the recent deaths of several of my friendships, such as the break with Paula, tormented me for a long time, as I repeatedly tried to understand why it came to this and what my own role was. And in writing this book, my interest is not merely in making generalizations about the pitfalls of the useful friendships that are so prevalent in the art world. Instead, my aim is to anchor my speculations on friendship within the personal in order to demonstrate how the challenges that confront this type of relationship are expressed within my own friendships, and how this can be represented as autofictional prose. My great role model in this respect is the German writer Marie Luise Kaschnitz, who succeeded in depicting personal experiences as events that go beyond the personal. At the same time, Kaschnitz characterized herself as a “perpetual auto-biographer,” a “writer trapped within her own circle.” This self-description is programmatically disparaging, as if it were a literary deficit for a writer to concern themselves with their immediate social environment. Kaschnitz often employed strategies of self-deprecation, possibly in the hope that her readers would tell her otherwise. But of course she deliberately opted for a form of writing that is grounded in the author’s own life-world, and therefore is powerful.

In essence, I hope to achieve something similar using different linguistic means: to examine the suprapersonal as a way of demonstrating how each self, including my own, is bound to others through friendship. This connection to others is not only positive; it also carries certain risks, as my own friendship dramas prove. By pointing out the enormous importance of friendship in my own life, I also counter the notion of an individual that exists “for itself”; in reality, we exist only in relation to others. The implications and consequences of this fundamental connection can be found within the phenomenon of friendship.

**10.23.2020**

My life has come to resemble a Shakespearean drama in recent days. Damning reviews of my newly published book,

*The Dark Years: Cologne, 1988–1999*, have been authored by friends of mine. While I knew they would write about my book, I assumed they would show me their reviews in advance, and maybe even discuss them with me before writing them. Instead, I now stumble across them, leaving me feeling as if I've been punched in the gut. While their words affect me, I also feel both guilty and outcast from their community. My book was evidently a serious (and irreparable) mistake on my part, for which I have now been punished with excommunication. I actually found some of their criticisms reasonable: they complain that I fixate on the scene's male protagonists, that I demystify this social universe instead of depicting it as a space of possibility, and that I sacrifice the political concerns of those involved by commodifying them and giving them over to the mainstream.

While these objections should be taken seriously, I can't escape the impression that in tearing my book to shreds, the authors also sought—unconsciously, I hope—to damage me personally. After all, their reviews signaled their desire to distance themselves from me and my work. In a field governed by the law of celebrity culture, it is impossible to separate these two things—that is, the product and the person behind it. Even the most objective criticism is taken as a personal attack. This is compounded by the fact that the tone of their reviews sounds self-righteous to my ears, as if they know something I've failed to grasp entirely. Their verdict seems to be: she's lost the plot. Why were they not more hesitant in their criticisms, instead of rejecting my book outright? For all its questionable aspects, which I too now recognize, might it not also contain some arguments that are worth considering, and maybe even defending?

I am particularly saddened that their virulent criticisms are gaining traction online, where they were greeted with applause, while my own attempt at acknowledging the mistakes and blind spots of my project in a publisher's statement was barely registered. I am currently experiencing on a smaller scale what it means to be "cancelled." On the one hand, cancelling is an important political weapon that helps marginalized and oppressed groups articulate their experiences of discrimination and publicly expose and pillory their all-powerful tormentors (à la Weinstein). At the same time, however, it is structured in such a way—as exemplarily demonstrated by Natalie Wynn on her ContraPoints channel on YouTube—that rejection of a particular individual comes to take the place of a justified repudiation of their actions or comments. And so, instead of strongly criticizing and refuting the transphobic statements made by someone like J. K. Rowling, the public declares Rowling herself to be a fundamentally bad person who needs to be cancelled. It is not my intention to draw a direct comparison between negative reactions to my book and the global shitstorm around Rowling (whose transphobic views I also find unacceptable), which makes the controversy around my book look like a storm in a teacup. But it does reflect the same tendency for criticism of a cultural product to tip over into defamation of the author online. Some have posted vicious attacks on me and my book on Facebook—posts that have been immediately commented upon by others who also show only disdain for me.

The readiness to cancel individuals deemed problematic is currently prevalent within the art world. Take the example of a recent conversation with a painter friend from New York. Whenever the names of the scene's male protagonists came up, she instantly asked, "But isn't he cancelled?" That her offhand question might actively contribute to this person being declared as finished didn't seem to worry her. Her suggestive question speaks of a social violence that has now become the norm. While there are cases where the expulsion of certain individuals is justified and extremely necessary (as with the #MeToo movement), to cancel someone in passing during a conversation is another matter.

But what conclusions can be drawn from the scathing reactions to my book with regard to the dynamics of friendship within a competitive society? Personally, I do not believe that loyalty is something that can be assumed in all situations, even from friendly colleagues. Intellectual or political conflicts can make it seem necessary for those who were previously allies to publicly distance themselves from one another. And yet I found the manner in which one of the authors defended her review to me over the phone today to be downright perverse. In no way had she wanted to stoke division against me and my book, she assurred me—on the contrary, her review was an expression of her "antagonistic solidarity." It was as if marking someone out for exclusion were the best path for support; as if division could be a method for fostering unanimity. In my view, it would have shown more solidarity—especially among friends—if she had discussed her criticisms with me in advance. I might have been able to convince her to adopt a less presumptuous tone in her text, and to opt for a less totalizing gesture—without this coming at the expense of her justified criticisms. Had I been informed in advance of her article, I could also have mentally prepared myself for its publication.

**10.24.2020**

I just spoke to my therapist about my friends' damning reviews of my book and the emotions they have triggered. In addition to feelings of loss and guilt, I am also filled with anger coupled with an irrational desire to retaliate. According to my therapist, there is a place for such aggression in my emotional life; the crucial thing is not to act on these desires. It's perfectly okay for me to sometimes crave revenge—just not to actually take it (nor would I really want to).

A further acquaintance whom I told about the negative reviews tried to put them down to envy on the part of my colleagues. They were bound to be jealous of my courage, she claimed, witnessing my attempt to break into new territory with my autobiographical account of the Cologne art scene. I rejected this interpretation, however, since it is both presumptuous and overly simplistic. I do not want to invalidate the justified criticisms of my colleagues by attributing them to a social affect such as envy, nor do I want to reduce the complex reasons behind them to a monocausal explanation. It is all too common for the valid claims of others (for greater inclusion, for example) to be written off as mere envy (or even social envy) by those in power. I don't want to make things so easy on myself, even if I don't necessarily feel as if I'm currently in any such position. For despite everything, it is important to me to take my friends' criticisms seriously without dismissing them as based on envy.

While it would be a mistake to explain my friends' behavior in such terms, none of us is immune to these feelings, as I myself know from experience. How often have I felt the stab of envy when others—including friends—seemed to receive more than I did. The sociologist Sighard Neckel recently traced the omnipresence of envy to the fact that humans are now "comparative beings": we constantly compare ourselves to others, and we mourn any recognition afforded to them that is denied to ourselves. This is all the more true since we live in a competitive society, whose "economic ethos," Neckel claims, is one of comparison. In other words, envy thrives particularly well within a milieu such as the art world, where merciless rivalry has always been the norm—it is therefore inevitable that an element of envy resonates within the attacks on my book, just as I am envious of the chorus of my critics, from which I feel excluded.

Situations in which I, too, have to battle back feelings of envy—I think here of conversations with my friend Phillip, for example—are far from rare. Phillip tends to offer me extensive, mostly monologic accounts of his latest academic successes, theoretical insights, and invitations to talk at prestigious institutions. Only rarely do I get a chance to speak in these conversations. In such moments I can sense envy welling up inside me, as I am left feeling that I have nothing comparable to report. While I am proud of my contribution to art-historical research, comparing it to his achievements makes me feel as if I'm going nowhere. I do attempt to chime in, sometimes even interrupting him to tell him of my current projects, without him having asked. And yet I find Phillip's rhetoric to be so overwhelming that I feel sidelined and belittled by him, and so I simply gaze in envy at the authority his work apparently enjoys. I do sometimes succeed in using this feeling productively, to spur me on with my own work. But I am generally left with a feeling of resignation; the vehemence with which he marks his territory forces me to capitulate and to realize and accept that my own accomplishments are more modest.

Neckel suggests that we might find a path out of envy by formulating our "own criteria" for a successful life instead of orienting ourselves toward those of others. The only problem with insisting on subjective criteria is that we live in a society centered on success, which imposes its criteria (like "having money") for what counts as a successful life upon us all. Here, it is hard for anyone to free themselves from the usual norms of success, certain aspects of which we have deeply internalized. For an academic to lack institutional recognition, for example, marks them as less successful than others. To defy these hierarchies and measure success and significance according to other criteria takes great strength.

**10.25.2020**

I don't know where to turn today. "Whereto am I?" I want to cry with Kaschnitz—where am I headed, what is my place, what should I be aiming for? Certain colleagues with whom I enjoyed friendly relationships have broken away from me in recent weeks, in part as a result of the furor around my book, leaving me feeling like I am in free fall, without a place in the world. I can only count myself lucky that because of corona there are currently no social events to attend, which would confront me with the shattered remains of some friendships. I anxiously picture future openings after the pandemic, the exhibition space a minefield. In my paranoid vision, every corner of the room is occupied by someone who either let me down or distanced themselves from me recently, with unfriendly, forbidding looks awaiting me wherever I turn. And yet I have spent my whole life avoiding situations where unresolved conflicts lurk around every corner. Whenever a rift has emerged with a friend or colleague, I always sought to talk it through in person, if only so I could continue to feel relaxed within my social environment. I now fear a future in which I spend long periods of time tangled in conflicts that can barely be separated from one another. The breaks and fault lines in these relationships can no longer be easily patched up, and my social life could soon resemble running the gauntlet. The map of friends and acquaintances I once had now seems out of date, and I have no idea what sort of social framework I can still count on. My exaggerated sense of social isolation causes me to devise escape scenarios in my head. What I need right now is distance, and I would love to take off for a place where the restructuring of my social life might appear less dramatic. But the rising infection rates mean that "non-essential travel" is strongly discouraged for the time being, and the neighborhood where I live has recently been declared as "high-risk," meaning closer refuges like the North Sea or Baltic coast are also out of the question. I am stuck here amid the ruins of my failed friendships, which seem to have piled up in recent weeks.

**12.5.2020**

In addition to the painful deaths of a number of my friendships, I have also—as should certainly be mentioned here—received a lot of support in recent weeks. Majorie, for example, called me every morning, or I her. While she, too, had problems with my book, she was outraged by how some of my friends tore it to pieces, and by the attacks against me online. Majorie helped me through this time, by attentively discussing these events with me for hours on end; the constant stream of new developments to be processed meant I often had to call and confer with her several times per day. When I was struggling with the question of what personal consequences this drama might have for me, she advised me to adopt an "open-door policy," meaning that I keep up the conversation with my opponents. And when it all became too much and I slipped into despondency over the harsh reactions to my book, she did her best to get me back on my feet.

I also experienced support from those who took an equally critical view of my literary experiment but rejected the severe reactions to it and personal defamations directed against me. Take the example of my artist friend Dominique, who considered my book to be problematic in political terms but still checked in on me several times a week, offering advice for how I might survive this period mentally and tactically.

In no way, then, was I actually alone, even if it felt that way during some dark moments.

Unfortunately, I tend to concentrate on the negative in my life, while I take positive experiences like the support of important friends or the few favorable and more encouraging reviews for granted. I fixate on my disappointments and injuries, painting a negative picture of my situation that ignores the good aspects, such as the fact that I can rely on my closest friends for support. This narrowing of perspective speaks of a false emphasis: I ultimately ascribe more importance to my professional life (and its pitfalls) than I do to my personal life. Even in times of domestic harmony, a professional crisis can bring me to my knees, as if my happiness were entirely dependent on positive developments in my career. That the support of my friends and family is not in itself capable of keeping my spirits aloft may also be because they seem outnumbered by my detractors. This perception may itself be a symptom of my fixation on the negative: I feel as if I am supported by few and challenged by many. And while my critics seem to speak their minds often and publicly, my supporters tend to shroud themselves in silence. As I perceive it, I have barely any backing and have been under attack since the publication of my book. "It's your own fault," my detractors seem to say, "that's the risk you take if you choose to publicly expose yourself with a popular historical account of the Cologne art world—you open yourself up to scrutiny in that social universe." And indeed, as someone with a certain degree of public presence, I probably do need to find a way to deal with occasionally functioning as a *Giftcontainer* (poison container), as Klaus Theweleit once described this existence—to have others project their self-hatred onto you while at the same time attracting toxicity yourself through your own mistakes.

Under these conditions, it's tempting to seek refuge among one's closest allies and avoid any public confrontation. A retreat of this sort would certainly have the advantage of taking me out of the line of fire. But it would also carry the risk of solipsism: to stay firmly within the circle of my supporters would mean no longer exposing myself to those harsh (but often justified) criticisms that question the validity of my project, and no longer integrating them into my thoughts and writing. I would then conduct my work from behind a protective wall, impermeable to any external influences. I want to avoid this at all costs; retreat is not an option. But in the future I will have to consider which situations I can expose myself to, and which will take too much of a toll on me.

**12.6.2020**

My friend Solange, to whom I gave the previous pages to read, has advised me to mediate more strongly between those passages where the discourse of abandonment dominates and those that chronicle enduring friendships. She's right; this book should not be just an indictment of lost (and instrumentally oriented) friendships or a mere hymn to intimate and dependable bonds.

In addition to the disappointments of recent times, I have also repeatedly experienced true friendship, as from Solange, who has remained loyal to me in times of crisis. It's not as if I am simply looking back on a trail of broken friendships; on the contrary, there were and are numerous friends—most recently Majorie—who call me up when they see I am attacked on social media to let me know how sorry they are. The worst aspect of cyberbullying is that even former allies can turn against you, making it feel as if you have been totally abandoned; it's as if open season had been declared on you, making you the target of a boundless hatred that you are ultimately unable to explain. What makes it worse is that almost no one steps in to condemn the haters and place themselves between you and them. In moments like these, when I drag myself through the day like a beaten dog, I am consoled by the empathetic words of my closest friends.

In her own reflections on friendship, Hannah Arendt already—like Schobin later on—declared conversation to be the medium within which such relationships are lived, claiming—and here I would agree with both Arendt and Schobin—that it represents the common social practice of friendship. The title of Sally Rooney's novel *Conversations with Friends* points in a similar direction: not only do conversations produce friendships, but it is through conversation that these relationships are tested and updated. Such exchanges presuppose the existence of a protected space where we may talk openly to our friend. Yesterday, I was once again made aware of how vital my conversations with Solange are, following a shared meal (indoors for once, at a good distance and next to open windows). Not only can I trust her with my gravest worries, fears, and anxieties, but we also celebrate the good things in our lives together, which are fortunately not infrequent. There is no resentment between us, and neither of us begrudges the other the good things she occasionally experiences. Should one of us feel the odd stab of envy upon hearing of the other's successes, we address it immediately. I do not fear that Solange will respond to the positive events in my life (whether great or small) with envy or animosity. These negative affects generally manifest themselves as an inability to participate—and by no stretch of the imagination can I detect any such incapacity in Solange.

Our conversations are characterized by lightning-fast shifts in register, seamlessly pivoting between the private and the professional; even our grievances are negotiated at high speed. In such moments, we will often state with satisfaction that "we've covered a lot of ground." We don't always find solutions in our conversations; at times we simply break out in laughter, providing some relief from the hopelessness of our situations (problems in our relationships, etc.). Laughing about these problems together robs them of their weight.

I make my way home from each dinner with Solange feeling lighter and more uplifted. As soon as I awake the next morning, I begin implementing her advice, often still in my pajamas; the fact that Solange has engaged with the details of my situation makes me feel more able to meet it. Her willingness and ability to empathize enables me to see myself through her eyes, and so to recognize the value of my own life. It suddenly seems worth continuing, and I find it easier to approach the problems I face. Without Solange's encouragement, I might have given up long ago.

**12.7.2020**

It would however be wrong to claim that my friendship with Solange is free of any instrumental streak. We often benefit from one another in our professional lives and sometimes actively lay the groundwork for each other's projects; the spectrum ranges from recommending reading material to advice regarding potential partners for future collaborations. And yet it is crucial that our relationship does not become subsumed by these "friendly favors" if its special quality is to be preserved. Our professional support for each other is just one of the pillars of our friendship; a far more stable foundation is our deep affection for one another. Were one of us to reorient herself in her career, or even withdraw from the art world entirely, this would not compromise the intimacy of our bond. With loving affection, we let the other know when we believe her to be taking the wrong path in her personal or professional life. In no way, then, do we simply endorse the life decisions of the other without questioning them; on the contrary, we also point out the possibly fatal consequences of our actions to each other. In doing so, the purpose is not merely to empathize, but also to observe the situation from a distance. Solange warns me when she considers me to be opening myself up to attack or taking unnecessary risks. Even if I don't share her reservations, I have to take them seriously, for she only has my protection in mind. Should she warn me against something, it is because she hopes to prevent me from falling into difficulties. While I have sometimes run into trouble after following the (often unintentionally) bad advice of some of my art-world friends, I can be sure that Solange always has my best interests at heart.

As already mentioned, we have also succeeded in keeping the feelings of envy that inevitably surface within any friendship in check. Should one of us enjoy a period of great happiness, when her life seems fabulous in every respect, then this is celebrated by the other, even when she herself is in crisis. This was the case when I met my partner nine years ago (we don't live together, which may be one of the reasons we manage to have a happy life as a couple). As I was experiencing the early period of rapturous and excessive infatuation with him, Solange was processing the heartbreak she felt when her own attempts at starting a new relationship proved unsuccessful. She made no secret of the fact that it was not easy for her to be confronted with my exhilarated state of mind. But she continued to support me in spite of this, and she was happy for me—not least since my situation gave her hope. If it was possible for me to have a fulfilling relationship, then Solange could also find someone.

For many years now, we have each been witness to the various phases of the other's life, following it with a mutual sense of goodwill and confirming that it has an impact and a value. Since my parents—the key witnesses to my life—have now been dead for several years, the sense of reassurance this friendship offers about my own existence is more precious than ever.

**12.8.2020**

My friendship with Solange serves as further proof that the old Aristotelian distinction between true, unselfish friendship and utility friendship is insufficient. Just as the borders between our private and personal lives became blurred in late modernity, it is no longer possible to draw a clear line between unselfish virtue friendships, as Aristotle called them, and utility friendships; on the contrary, the two mostly merge into one another.

This conflation of self-interest and selflessness within friendships carries new risks. I myself have been disappointed by numerous art-world friendships that I hoped were virtuous—that is, when I have wanted to be valued for who I am. It was painful and disillusioning to see what I considered to be an unselfish virtue friendship reveal its true face—that of a primarily instrumental relationship. And the same must be true for friends of mine who believed they were valued for their personalities, and who at some point realized our friendship was shaped by considerations of its potential benefits. That esteem for the other and selfish expectation are amalgamated within the friendly bond is something those involved are often conscious of. In this light, my friendship with Solange is unusual in that it does not depend on its usefulness; the fact that we are able to help each other in our careers is a side effect of our friendship, not its raison d'être. Far more significant is the fact that we have committed ourselves to one another regardless of the benefits. The core of our friendship is an ethical commitment to each other, independent of any considerations of usefulness. This pact may be rescinded at any point, of course—the moment the behavior of the friend radically contradicts one's own ethical principles, for example. But since both Solange and I follow a similar moral compass, it's unlikely we will fall out in this way.

In fact, my trust in Solange runs so deep that I would grant her power of attorney if I became ill. Although even trust is not free of usefulness, as Martin Hartmann has demonstrated. Despite its "intrinsic value," he claims, trust is nonetheless fundamentally instrumental, if only because it allows for the realization of other values. Without trust, friendship would have no value, and goods would not be traded on the market. It is therefore not free of utility or indeed of purpose; on the contrary, it is oriented toward practices that are dependent upon precisely such considerations.

What are the implications of this for the bond that exists between me and Solange? While the trust I show her has a value of its own, it simultaneously enables something as useful as our friendship. Analogous to our friendship, then, our trust for one another also has an instrumental streak. According to Hartmann, what characterizes friendship's "practice of trust" is that it prioritizes sameness over difference; he claims we tend to show trust toward those whose feelings and actions we consider to be "appropriate." It is thus only the existence of certain attitudes and practices that allows for the development of trust.

The notion that trust is socially contingent by nature is certainly true of me and Solange: while our backgrounds differ in terms of class, we operate within the same ethical framework, share fundamental convictions (regarding friendship, for example), and each act in a way that is relatable to the other.

It's also possible that our shared institutional context (academia and art criticism) makes it easier for us to build a bond of trust: we can judge each other's actions more effectively, and we find ourselves confronted with similar questions and problems. It's therefore logical that I have rarely developed comparably trusting relationships with those from entirely different contexts, since the trust essential to friendship thrives under shared institutional conditions. But this also means that both trust and friendship have an exclusory element: should someone's professional context be totally unfamiliar, I am less likely to become close to them. The chances that I will enter a deep friendship with this person are thus reduced.

**12.14.2020**

Reading Derrida's book *The Politics of Friendship*, I came across what might be described as friendship's sociopolitical dimension. Invoking Aristotle, Derrida relates friendship to democracy: democracy requires a community, and the latter is inconceivable without friendship. Democracy and friendship are therefore mutually related: without friendship there can be no democracy, and the absence of democracy hampers the conditions of friendship. Given this connection, it's no surprise that both democracy and friendship are currently experiencing difficulties. Democracy is threatened by the rise of right-wing populist movements, and the principle of friendship is being emptied out above all online, where friends are no longer friends. And of course, the success of contemporary right-wing populism is also in part a result of digital forms of communication, where personal attacks, resentment, and uninhibited bullying are the order of the day.

In writing this book, my intention is not merely to trace the manifold erosions friendship is currently experiencing—both online and offline—but also to sing the praises of friendship under adverse conditions, and to devise strategies for its continued survival. From a Derridean standpoint, my vindication of friendship may also be understood as a defense of democracy at a time when it is under threat. Such a reading would be entirely in keeping with my own understanding of friendship—as the prototype of a community that is conducive to democracy.

**12.15.2020**

My comments must be supplemented with the aspect of care for one's friends. Within the artistic field, there are in fact certain social contexts where unconditional loyalty and care are common. Here, I am thinking of a group of acquaintances who, a few years ago, came together to support a friend who was seriously ill with leukemia; they looked after him, regularly visiting and caring for him up until his death. Their entire social circle organized itself around their friend turned patient: visits were coordinated among one another, their friend was accompanied to medical appointments, and they shared in his hopes and fears. And when his condition eventually deteriorated, they dropped all professional and personal commitments so they could be with him in his final hours.

Most of these people had maintained a close working relationship with this friend. And yet in no way did they turn away from him when he became weaker and unable to work; on the contrary, they spent a great deal of time with him, reading to him and so forth. The engagement this group showed for their sick friend was not oriented around utility but instead came close to the Aristotelian ideal of true, unselfish friendship. At the same time, their dedication can also be seen as having carried unintended benefits: belonging to this circle of helpers conferred a certain nobility upon the members of the group, and their relationships with one another were strengthened by their shared focus on their friend. Yet it would be wrong to suggest that their primary interest was in benefiting from his illness; far more important is that this group rallied around their friend, like an extended family. They also supported one another in dealing with the enormous psychological burden that comes with accompanying a friend at the end of his life.

The engagement of this group testifies to the fact that friendships have taken on familial functions; here, it was a community of friends that provided the care that would once have been the primary preserve of family members. Of course, even such progressive and caring friendship groups as theirs are not free of power struggles, hierarchies, and aggressions. But friendship in the case of illness, in contrast to the principle of the utility friendship, means taking responsibility for one another. While there were isolated examples of such practices of care among friends in the artistic milieus of the nineteenth and twentieth centuries, it is now quite common to encounter friendship groups of this sort who rally around and care for friends when they are ill. While the sick person cannot be "useful" in instrumental terms, they do not turn away; instead, they ensure their friend does not die alone.

**12.16.2020**

Derrida addresses circles of friends or friendships with many in *The Politics of Friendship*. He points out that ethical friendship as understood by Aristotle was dependent on its rarity. Since antiquity, friendship has only ever been eulogized as something between two individuals (who, naturally, were always imagined to be men); any more than two friends would be out of the question for an ethical friendship. To limit the concept of friendship to two people is barely conceivable today; instead, we now observe an inflation of "friends," above all on online platforms. That friendly contacts now represent an economic resource is also due to the "networking" imperative of the neoliberal economy: the more of them we have, the greater the advantages they offer for advancing our careers. In a networked economy, such contacts are therefore known to be worth their weight in gold.

Measured against the Aristotelian ideal of friendship as something rare, I myself have too many friends (despite their number reducing after my book came out). According to Aristotle, to have numerous friendships comes at the cost of their uniqueness, since unique (i.e., singular) friendships cannot exist in multiplicity. And indeed, it can be upsetting to realize that a close friend maintains numerous other intimate friendships. If I were to find out that Majorie has several friends to whom she is as close as she is to me, it would relativize the intensity of our bond slightly; conversely, there are friends of mine who have to deal with the fact that there are others to whom I am similarly close. In principle, friendship should not be thought of in terms of possession. But it is not always easy to share a close friend with others, even if I am happy for her that she has so many friends. Moreover, in encountering these friends of friends, I meet new people who might enrich my own life.

Derrida also took the view that the proliferation of friendship need not threaten its exclusivity. Instead, he focused on the possibility of inclusive multiple friendships by inverting the usual understanding of Aristotle's (supposed) exclamation "O my friends, there is no friend." He saw it not as a lament about the absence of any friend at the end of the philosopher's life, but as a plea for a life with many friends ("O my friends"). According to Derrida, Aristotle's ostensible regret at having "no friend" belies the fact that he advocated a pluralization of friendship. Based on this interpretation, Derrida developed an expanded concept of friendship that ultimately approaches his political ideal of "hospitality"—that is, of also treating strangers as if they were friends. I see the great strength of Derrida's more inclusive concept of friendship as lying in its break with the exclusionary and exclusive tradition of friendship as something that only exists between two men.

At the same time, Derrida's preference for the "many" also appears in a different light today, in view of the inflation of friendship on social media. Our online friends are as countless as they are exchangeable, and so it would be entirely inappropriate to talk of "obligations" to them in this context. Given the fundamentally replaceable nature of these online friends, it might seem entirely reasonable to return (contra Derrida) to Aristotle's notion of the rare value of true friends in our analog lives whom we value for their unique characters. After all, to have just a few true friends need not mean closing oneself off to others and staying within one's own bubble. It is possible to cultivate one's unique friendships while also living Derrida's ideal of hospitality; it simply means doing justice to two different types of friendship simultaneously, without playing them against one another.

**12.18.2020**

I recently came across an interesting study about the art world in the 1960s that claims it was not an artist's work that was pivotal in achieving institutional recognition but the number of friends and international contacts they had: the more international and global their network, the better their chances of commercial success. It was the same in the early 1990s, and I have no reason to think that the situation today is different. For ideally, having friends means they will promote you or recommend you to market agents. That it is above all through "personal recommendations" that "trust in the abilities of the work subject" is established throughout society at large is demonstrated by Andreas Reckwitz in his book *The Society of Singularities*; here, such recommendations serve as the means for building confidence and value alike. The same is true of the informal economy of the art world, where institutional attention and recognition often comes down to the support of an artist's colleagues.

Backroom politics of this sort have been one of the field's most enduring rituals since the early modern period. Since the 1990s, however, what was once a limited milieu (in terms of size, at least) has metamorphosized into a global industry governed by unfettered competition and pitiless rivalry. In my observation, this structural transformation has affected the principle of recommendation to the extent that friends are often not recommended since they also represent potential competitors. Instead, the tendency is now to support unknown and distant colleagues, since a new professional contact seems to offer greater rewards. To pass over a friend when making such recommendations also has the advantage of taking them out of the running as a prospective rival; in my own experience, it was often some of my close colleagues who overlooked my work or failed to invite me to conferences related to my research topics. They have also ignored my publications while leaping upon comparable texts by colleagues whom they did not know personally. While they were happy to issue recommendations and invitations for the others, they seemed to take my position for granted.

I myself am not free of this reluctance to recommend friends. Instead of doing the obvious—that is, endorsing the valued work of a friend or colleague—I too am more likely to support someone whom I do not know personally in certain situations. Beyond the latent element of competitiveness, there are other reasons for my hesitancy to suggest friends for jobs: I don't want to attract any accusations of favoritism, for one thing, and my support for a friend might represent a threat to our friendship. Should our personal and professional relationships become intertwined, any dispute we experience in our careers might also spell the end of our friendship. Furthermore, to work with a friend makes conflicts inevitable on the personal level.

It is therefore often a deliberate decision not to bring a friend into play in such situations, even when they would be a perfect fit for the role—and this for the sake of our friendship. The extent to which my own sense of competition plays a role in such decisions is hard to judge in retrospect. Or is it simply too hard for me to admit to myself that I, too, am capable of competitive behavior?

**12.19.2020**

I dreamed of my friends and my sister in various constellations last night. What the situations had in common was that I was deprived from participating in them: while I made dogged attempts to get involved and pleaded with them to "let me in," they ignored me, and I remained outside. The others were together, while my lot was that of the loner. First to appear was my ex-boyfriend Carl, who was busy talking to friends and ignored me, despite me clamoring for his attention. I then came upon my sister Silvia, who was also surrounded by friends and did not deign to look at me; like Carl before her, she too let me know that her friends were more important to her than I was at this moment.

That both dream fragments circled around the theme of social exclusion seems to me no coincidence. Last night I spoke to a colleague—author of one of the damning reviews—whom I used to count among my friends but now barely trust. Following our frosty conversation, I must have (unconsciously) feared that not only would she turn against me but her entire social circle would too. In addition to its paranoia, my dream pointed to another issue: the futility of my persistent battle for attention and inclusion, which I have waged since childhood. Even my father's favor could only be won through exceptional achievement and maintaining an image that was as radiant as possible. He rarely showed any interest in me for my own sake; I always had to do something to earn it. In the art world, too, I first had to pass through numerous initiation rituals before I could belong; I ran the risk of being left out if I didn't bang my own drum as loudly as possible. The dream also speaks to my fear of what might happen if I made no such efforts—perhaps I'd find myself excluded. Deep down, I am convinced that no one will pay me any attention if I don't actively put myself in the picture.

In response to the dream, I resolve to refrain from constantly setting off fireworks in the future, and to instead just wait and see what happens if I stop trying so hard. While the possibility that things will come to a standstill fills me with anxiety, it's better than spending a lifetime doing somersaults. Perhaps my dream also wanted me to experience some of the pain I inflicted upon my sister when I made her feel she was less important to me than my friends. How many times I relegated her to second or third place! And it was there that I found myself in my dream, whose lesson was twofold: this is how it feels to be simply ignored, and stop being so desperate to be heard and included. Just do nothing for once and let what happens happen.

**12.20.2020**

The more progress I make with this text, the more I worry about how my friends and former friends will react when the book comes out. How will they feel about me drawing upon my relationships with them, even if in fictionalized form? The thought that it might cause a minor shitstorm fills me with anxiety. The tension I feel when I picture the potentially negative reactions of my friends leaves me unable to write any further. I am unfit to work. This tension fills me to my core, physically manifesting itself as a painful pressure in my lower back, and I sit at my desk as if paralyzed. I feel a rush of regret rising within me in such moments, a sense of shame that I am using my friends and my experiences with them for this project. Is it not downright perfidious of me to write a book on the instrumental nature of art-world friendships while at the same time doing that very thing myself—using my friendships as material for this book? Or is there simply no getting around the contradiction that my critique of instrumental friendship also means exploiting both these relationships and other, less useful friendships? This contradiction seems to be constitutive for the project. Its fictive aspects are interwoven with the personal, and forgoing references to my own experiences of friendship would diminish its power. After all, the thoughts it presents were triggered by events in my own life. It takes a specific viewpoint to breathe life into sociological observation.

There are also methodological reasons why I cannot afford to omit the personal. In undertaking this project, I resolved to close the gap between its analytical and emotional layers, which are normally strictly separated. I'm interested in how social upheavals and the new pressures they create find expression within individual friendships, and in our individual feelings about friendship. The point is therefore to examine the power of those structures that influence my affective behavior (and that of my friends). Social structures may also be differently negotiated within the framework of a friendship, to the benefit of true and gratifying friendship. The question that concerns me most is how fulfilling, lifelong friendships can be nurtured in the face of such difficult conditions.

The art establishment might react especially strongly to my attempt to demystify its friendships. Its actors cling to the belief that they are actually friends with their business partners—and all in the name of art. I recently came across a statement that is symptomatic in this respect, in which a collector characterizes her relationship to a curator she employs as an "unshakeable friendship." This romanticized view of their relationship—collector and curator, united in their love of art—ignores its precarious aspect, with one person dependent on the other. That such exaggerated expectations are now placed upon friendship is, in my view, partly due to the disenchantment of romantic love, whose economic character can no longer be doubted in the face of such different cultural phenomena as Tinder and the studies on the economy of romantic love by Eva Illouz. Perhaps friendship fills the void left by the demystification of romantic love: friendship functions as a beacon of hope, and we project our longing for supportive relationships onto it. Seen this way, friendship operates entirely under the logic of capitalism. But no one wants to give up the final ground where we may act unselfishly and with consideration for others. The same is true for me.

**12.21.2020**

I had another friendship dream last night. This time, the theme was my fear of being too close to my friends and the associated loss of control. I pack my suitcase, ensuring I'm prepared for every eventuality. Possible changes of weather, sporting activities, dinners that require an elegant outfit—all these situations are considered when selecting my clothes. I pack for a three-day journey by ship that was organized together with some friends. Once on board, I discover an old friend from my youth, who informs me that the ship will be sailing not for three days but a minimum of ten. I have only packed for three, however, and after thinking it over for a moment, I decide to disembark; I'm neither willing nor able to enter such an experiment, and certainly not without the right wardrobe.

The idea of undertaking a journey in company equipped with such a meagre selection of clothing seems unthinkable to me. The option of borrowing clothes from friends on this journey is also not something I relish, since I associate this dependency with a loss of control. At no cost do I want to go without my carefully assembled outfits—my protective armor. To me, the idea of wearing other people's clothes carries the danger of opening myself up to attack, of no longer being myself, of losing myself.

As soon as I have decided to leave the ship, I feel a sense of relief. The prospect of spending days on end stuck on a ship with some of my friends, with no chance of escape, fills me with panic; their company needs to be enjoyed in measured doses, and I only have a limited capacity for engaging with it. I want to be able to retreat to the seclusion of my study after our meetings, where I have things (more or less) under control. During our voyage, by contrast, I would be entirely at their mercy—at every meal and during every activity. Imagining their permanent presence triggers a sort of pre-burnout in me: an anticipated sense of exhaustion and depression. To embark on this journey would take me far beyond my comfort zone. I'd rather stay home at my desk.

The message of this dream seems to be that I am unable to fully abandon myself to the adventure of friendship. If being with my friends prevents me from continuing to live as I am used to, I retreat. Does my dream imply I am incapable of true friendship, since it requires us to risk involving ourselves in the otherness of others? In truth, my thirst for adventure is limited, and I seem to be anything but flexible. The mere prospect of a group trip is enough for me to break out in a cold sweat; it's for this reason that I always book a single room when traveling with friends, as a matter of course.

There is another "truth," however, which I have suppressed until now, and which (seemingly) contradicts what is outlined above: I am extremely open to new friendships, and particularly in unfamiliar situations, such as conferences spread over multiple days. My attitude to friendship is riddled with contradictions. Despite my strong need for solitude, I am also open to meeting new people, as is apparent when I'm attending a multiday symposium in an unfamiliar city. Such events display certain parallels to life on board the ship in my dream: you're never alone, and you have to adapt to unforeseen events. For academics, these conferences also serve as an opportunity to make friends with colleagues. I have often entered ad hoc conference friendships, whose special quality is that they rarely outlive the event in question. If the conference is hosted in an out-of-the-way location, the connection to the other participants can become quite intense. Most of the time I enjoy this intensity, since it inevitably brings surprises and can sometimes have an erotic undertone; indeed, I have often witnessed colleagues tumble into an affair at a conference. As if on a school trip, regressive alliances also emerge between certain participants, with all decisions, such as planning the day's activities, subsequently made together: Should we go for a walk, or should we listen to the next presentation? It's as if, for the duration of the conference, you were living with someone you actually barely know.

Upon arrival at a conference, I am immediately on the lookout for potential allies with whom—if the pact is successful—I can sit during every meal. While a fast friendship at these events can sometimes be the result of shared academic interests, it's often simply based on sympathy. The participant one gets on best with at a conference can be the person with whom one has little in common in terms of work; what makes them appealing is their habitus or lifestyle. After spending the evening in the bar, come morning the battered participants reunite over breakfast in the hotel dining room. They share each other's exhaustion, and experiencing one another in this sleepy state generates a sense of intimacy; to be constantly in each other's company produces a familiarity that would otherwise take years to develop. In my experience, friendships and allegiances of this sort are formed at every conference—it seems to be an anthropological law of such events. To discuss the latest presentation with a like-minded colleague over coffee during the break simply makes it easier to survive a stressful symposium and its nonstop barrage of information.

There is a point at which these alliances have their fate decided: when the time comes for the conference friends to give their presentations. Whether the speaker discredits themselves in the eyes of the others or unbridgeable rifts emerge among the group as a result of a presentation or a comment, friendship dramas unfold at a dynamic pace. It often takes no more than a positive or disparaging remark about a participant's talk for new friendships and enmities to form; even more so than with ordinary utility friendships, conference friendships may be terminated at any time. Even a critical follow-up question can sound the death knell for a conference friendship. For this question is no small matter to the speaker; in the worst case, they could see it as discrediting their work. Previous feelings of friendship are thus transformed into their opposite, since this potential conference friend has now revealed themselves to be an academic opponent.

### 1.9.2021

According to Roland Barthes's biographer Tiphaine Samoyault, all that remained at the end of the French thinker's life was his friends. When he no longer had the safety net of structuralism, semiology, and Marxism to fall back on, it was they who protected him—the intellectual trapeze artist—from crashing to earth. While his friends made up for the lost schools of thought, I wonder whether his departure from these established doctrines might also have had the opposite effect: by breaking with them, Barthes could have distanced himself from those friends who wanted to continue to cling to their orthodoxies. Some of Barthes's political friends undoubtedly resented the fact that he showed barely any support for the protest movements of May 1968. Having experienced the death of his mother, he dreamed instead of a different and less academic form of writing; he imagined a new life, a *vita nova*, and gave lectures on "The Preparation of the Novel." Barthes died in 1980, and his novel was never written. And yet while it never got further than the preparatory stage, the goal had been set.

I can empathize with Barthes's situation, above all with the sense of dissatisfaction he felt toward academic writing (his disinterest in new protest movements, by contrast, I do not share). Like Barthes, I too felt an urge to find a new way of writing following the deaths of my parents; to move away from an academic tone but without forgoing scholarly reflections entirely. I longed to write more freely, and for a theoretical reflection that gave greater weight to the personal and the affective. But unlike Barthes, the heyday of my friendships—and this is especially true of my utility friendships—correlated with the artistic and political project I pursued in the early 1990s together with my friends. We were united in our battle against the renewed racism and sexism of that period, and we were bound together by the fact that we all supported certain artistic practices that were located somewhere between institutional critique and conceptual painting. Today, by contrast, we would find it hard to agree on the merits of even one individual artist's work. And while it's clear to all of us that the enemy stands to the right, and that wokeness and identity politics are, in principle, to be defended, there are now constant political schisms among my left-wing friends, formed around an ever-shifting front line.

My loss is therefore a double one: a shared political project and some friendships that accompanied it. While Barthes compensated for his departure from certain schools of thought with his friendships, the plurality of approaches, methods, and political convictions among my own friends has served to weaken some of our relationships. There are certain friends with whom I now lack the ideological cement that once kept us together; we no longer share each other's goals as we once did. Naturally, I remain close to some of these friends—either because we have succeeded in overcoming our intellectual or political differences or because we can agree on certain essentials, which we constantly renegotiate according to the situation. By continually renewing the ideational foundation of our friendship, our bond becomes ever deeper and more intimate.

Analogous to love (per Theweleit), friendship, too, is work. As with Samoyault's description of Barthes, my remaining friends offer me a certain stability. But as to whether they would actually be my safety net … here, the metaphor of the trapeze artist overlooks the reality of my life. For my friends (fortunately) have other things to do than protect me; ultimately, it is down to me to ensure I stay balanced on the trapeze and do not fall.

**1.10.2021**

A few days ago, I gave the first fifty pages of this manuscript to an agent to read (we are also friends, naturally). She was very complimentary about them, including their literary quality, and she's agreed to support my book. I can barely contain my joy. With a renewed sense of self-confidence—and not without a certain hubris—I wonder if I might be in the process of becoming a fiction writer. It gives me an enormous boost to know that she approves of my manuscript.

I'm currently contemplating how I might best maintain the narrative tension until the end, and how the whole thing can be concluded without becoming long-winded. Further aspects constantly force their way into my thoughts—including at night—which I faithfully record in my notebook. The tempo of my writing has increased; I approach the task with more courage and confidence than before, and I no longer torture myself with questions of whether this project is sensible or interesting enough to be worth pursuing. But might it be very dangerous to no longer doubt the legitimacy of this project? I am concerned that the book will now fall into two halves: the first of them penned in a state of disillusion and dejection, and the second underpinned by enthusiasm and optimism. Does my text perhaps need the despondency of its early pages if it is to be urgent and necessary to the reader? Or do these thoughts simply reproduce the old cliché of the productive unhappiness of the author?

It might have been better to wait until the manuscript is finished before giving it to my agent friend. Her positive reaction has affected my psychological state; I now feel strangely nervous and skittish, flustered by her encouragement and unable to concentrate. I suddenly find myself spending a great deal of time imagining the book's possible future as a glittering success. The hope has taken root that I might earn more money from my writing; that my attempt at working as both author and critic might pay off in financial terms. At this point images start tumbling through my head: I see myself—like Knausgaard—in a stately residence, my days spent writing, occasionally taking breaks to jump into the pool. But then I return to the present, and I remind myself of the reality of my life: while I am reasonably privileged and financially secure, my bank balance is notoriously low. A villa or even a vacation home is out of my reach. To lead a satisfied life might also come at a cost to my writing, were all my material dreams fulfilled. That it might be this book that makes this dream a reality is far from likely. But my agent has put ideas in my head with her enthusiasm.

**1.12.2021**

It became clear to me today that I must further refine the concept of utility friendship—above all in view of my friend Evelyne, whom I spoke to yesterday on the phone. Evelyne is an exceptional figure among my artist friends: she is extremely open and interested in other people, with an empathetic outlook and a ready willingness to help others when they fall into difficulties. Viewed from the outside, one might take our friendship to be a classic utility friendship between a (recognized) critic and a (successful) artist. The reality is more complicated, however.

First and foremost, I am the one who benefits from this friendship, and in several respects. Since she is an internationally respected and commercially successful artist, our close, longlasting, and trusting relationship bolsters my own symbolic value in the art establishment. It is often the case that curators will turn to me when they want to reach Evelyne. My task in such instances is to fend them off, which I do with Evelyne's permission and in her interests. She lives a secluded life in the South of France and wishes to be bothered as little as possible, and she refuses to give interviews. And so I help her to erect a sort of cordon around herself, thus ensuring she remains unreachable.

What distinguishes Evelyne from other successful artists is that she has no interest in becoming even more successful. She does not seek to expand her career, and she does not feel compelled to increase her earnings; on the contrary, she often passes up lucrative offers since she feels she already has enough money. She trenchantly defends her freedom against outside pressures. I have always found her lack of self-importance to be a relief. While she is naturally proud of her accomplishments, she also knows that success is not based on achievement alone and requires an element of luck. Success is not something that is generated entirely by oneself; it is also a result of social conditions and chance. For this reason, Evelyne takes herself and her work less seriously than many other artists do.

A key feature of our friendship is her generosity toward me, and she never expects any service in return. There is a silent agreement between us that I will not support her professionally: I don't write catalogue texts for her, and I don't give talks on her work. She, by contrast, showers me with gifts. Evelyne includes those around her in her success, and she allows herself to be generous without keeping a tally of whether she's received anything in return. I, on the other hand, am unable to free myself from these calculations; I am sometimes stressed by the fact that I can offer so little in return—on a material level, at least. At the same time, I am available to her in every facet of my person. During long phone calls, we cover a wide spectrum of topics ranging from health problems to professional decisions to what each of us is reading. Evelyne is among those artists who are more comfortable when discussing subjects other than their work. Should I bring up one of her exhibitions—which happens only rarely, since I know she is reluctant to discuss them—she becomes monosyllabic. She is much more interested in psychology, films, books, and the personalities of certain authors and academics, such as Niklas Luhmann or Michel Houellebecq, including how they present themselves in public talks.

That Evelyne routinely steers the conversation away from her work speaks to her refreshingly un-self-centered nature. One might interpret her (seeming) disinterest in her own work as a sign of sovereignty—that she does not want to force the topics that interest her onto others. I also think her work benefits from the fact that her thinking does not revolve around it entirely. That she does not play the role of the obsessed artist corresponds to her artwork's nonchalant multimedia aesthetic. Instead, she seems to see every conversation and every encounter as a chance not to have to think about her own work, to leave it at the door. She also has a sense of what an imposition self-centered narcissistic monologues are for the listener. Her enthusiasm for subjects beyond art means that conversations with her are always easy and relaxing—she gets by without self-promotion. I, on the other hand, occasionally find myself referring to a book or text of mine. I resolve to avoid doing so in the future.

Rereading this entry, I realize I am in danger of glorifying Evelyne, of elevating her to a beacon of light with whom I share a "perfect, inviolate, and entire" bond à la Montaigne. He, too, idealized his connection to Étienne de La Boétie as a friendship beyond utility—one unsullied by unrelated motives like "purpose" or "profit." Montaigne also emphasized the exceptional nature of their bond, since he considered such relationships a rarity "amongst the men"—only men, once again—of his age. Like Aristotle before him, who declared the true friend to be a "second self," Montaigne invoked a "perfect unity" between friends; as one soul in two bodies, they can "neither lend nor give anything to one another." Thankfully, Evelyne and I are a long way from such a symbiosis, and our souls remain our own. It is precisely because we approach each other as distinct individuals that we are able to enter into an exchange, and that we can give each other gifts.

While I stand by my admiration for Evelyne's readiness to support others, I should add that her generosity does have its limits, and that its benefits are not enjoyed by everyone. She often rejects the countless requests for a work of hers, and she does not support every charitable initiative. Some members of the art establishment would also describe her very differently than I have—possibly as "peculiar" or "difficult." I have the advantage of extreme familiarity because of our long-lasting acquaintance. Our friendship seems—see here Montaigne—to belong to a different time, since unlike most connections in the art world, it is not based on the principle that "one hand washes the other." I think we reward each other—her me more than I her—for the fact we are connected by a long, shared history. We know each other so well that we are able to have a conversation without having to clarify much in advance, and we are aware of each other's idiosyncrasies. Evelyne's generosity seems to be her way of celebrating our deep mutual understanding; her magnanimity is an expression of a bond that carries no agenda.

**1.13.2021**

To know someone for many years can also often have the opposite effect, since long-term friends frequently take each other for granted and fail to make an effort with one another. This was possibly true of Peter and me: while we felt we knew each other well, we each held the other to an image we formed of them several decades ago, barely acknowledging that they might have developed since—as if we had long ago checked them off our list. We invested more energy in forging new ties while treating each other like old relatives: typical Isabelle, typical Peter! In reality, the images we had of each other were long in need of an update. It was probably sheer laziness that prevented us from engaging with one another more deeply. Had we done so, we may have registered the manifold changes we have both undergone since we first met.

It was particularly painful for me to witness the effort Peter made with new acquaintances at openings, while he seemed to only greet me in passing, leaving me standing like an old piece of furniture he was no longer interested in. I realized in such moments just how good he is at winning people over—an engagement that I always felt was lacking in our own relationship. Then again, it's possible he perceived my own behavior in a similar way. Perhaps I, too, had chalked him up as a reliable asset that no longer required any intensive maintenance. This negligence on both sides might have led to our break.

Today, I feel the dissolution of our friendship was necessary in order for us to come together again on a new footing. There were weeks of silence between us, and I was saddened that he made no effort to reestablish contact with me. Then, yesterday, our paths crossed at an exhibition, for which we had each coincidentally booked the same "time slot," as is necessary during the pandemic. We immediately fell into conversation about the paintings and objects on display; it was as if the torn thread of our communication was instantly repaired, as if our exchanges on art had never been interrupted. However, it was initially unclear which role we had assumed: Former friends now engaging in a friendly professional conversation, or ex-friends glossing over and ignoring their actual separation? I think it was less a case of us repressing our split and more that we wanted to reassure ourselves that we could continue to have productive conversations about art, even without maintaining a close friendship. We quickly entered our usual mode of brainstorming: we agreed on the strengths and weaknesses of the exhibition, on the historical references within the paintings, and on the highlights and lowlights among the exhibited works. We also addressed the exhibition architecture in detail, relating it to previous displays at the same institution—the Hamburger Bahnhof—and agreeing that the current installation was more successful. Finally, we discussed the dangers involved in the artist's painting procedures along with the great potential of her approach. In between, we pointed out certain morphological details in the paintings or humorous work titles.

Hours passed as we strolled through the museum chatting away. The curator attempted to join our conversation at one point, but without success; we were simply too tuned into one another to tolerate any interruption from outside. At the end of this unexpected encounter our paths parted, and we each made our way home without going for a coffee first. That the cafés were closed due to the lockdown suited us perfectly, since to engage in such a ritual would still have been inappropriate for our relationship as it stood. After all, we had encountered one another at the exhibition by coincidence and as ex-friends—ex-friends who made an ad hoc attempt to transform their former friendship into a productive encounter. To attempt to revive our previous camaraderie in a café would have been a step too far. In retrospect, I am amazed at how comfortable we were with each other—without discussing it, we seemed to have agreed on a functional mode of exchange. We are clearly still greatly interested in one another, despite our separation, for why else would we have spent hours together at the exhibition?

Thinking about this encounter with Peter, I begin to see the positive effects of our split. That I felt forced to show him the red card might have strengthened my position, not least since I formulated my point of view unambiguously and showed resolve; I demonstrated that I would not allow myself to be mistreated by him, that my own well-being is more important than our strategically useful friendship. It became clear yesterday that this break has had a positive effect on his behavior: he seemed far more polite and respectful than before. Perhaps the ending of our friendship was—paradoxically—the only way to save it in the longer term. I greatly hope it can be continued—on different terms and in a different form.

**1.18.2021**

If a friendship is dominated by its instrumental dimension, then it is easier to replace the friend in question. For if they were primarily chosen to fulfill a task, it is their function that is of paramount importance, and this may be taken over by someone else. I am currently experiencing this painfully with Peter, who is now close to Sabine, an artist friend of mine. Although he had little to do with her before our split, they are now seemingly best friends. This might sound like a playground drama, but it's irritating nonetheless. When Peter recently celebrated his birthday, he chose to spend it alone with Sabine because of the lockdown, as she reported to me today in an email—and not without some pride. In doing so, he demonstrated that I am no longer in the picture. Ending my friendship with him has shaken up our circle of friends, which is now shifting and constituting itself anew. While it's only natural for Peter to partner up with someone else in the course of this restructuring, it also serves as my (possibly unintended) symbolic punishment: should someone leave the circle, new alliances are formed and the defector is isolated. At the same time, I am also seeking new alliances, and Peter may equally feel that I have replaced him with other artist friends.

Peter also succeeded in filling the position of authorized art historian delegated with representing his art—and with Solange, of all people. She told me over the phone this morning that he asked her to write a catalogue text for him. I encouraged her to write it, but also admitted that it stung me slightly to be superseded in this way. While others might have a more relaxed response, events from my childhood make it painful to feel I am being “replaced” by someone else. As a one-year-old I was confronted with the birth of my sister, thus challenging my exclusive place by my parents’ side, and my father replaced my mother (with a much younger woman, naturally) just three months after they finalized their divorce—and without including us in his new life. Replacement trauma in every direction.

I therefore have a special antenna for the replacement politics of others. If it’s so easy for Peter to transfer my previous function to other people, I was probably right in thinking that his interest in me was primarily motivated by functional considerations; he likely valued me above all for my usefulness to him. And yet I am stunned by the speed at which he has replaced me with others. This is what my therapist predicted back when I was first considering breaking off my friendship with Peter. But I didn’t believe her; I thought she was being unfair to him, making assumptions that were unjustified. It’s a crushing realization that she was correct. In principle, I am aware that each of us is replaceable—myself included. But to experience it in practice is decidedly uncomfortable. Perhaps I should remind myself of this pain in the future, in those moments when I, too, catch myself practicing the politics of replacement.

**1.19.2021**

In the art world, it is advisable to aim for a modus vivendi with one's ex-friends that is acceptable to all sides, since repeated encounters—often over several decades—are inevitable. For a generation of artists to become fully institutionalized takes forty years on average, and it is impossible to avoid meeting ex-friends or supposed opponents during this long period of time. It would certainly have been advisable for me to talk things through with my fiercest critics and former friends following the negative reviews of my book. This is easier said than done, however, since vulnerability makes it hard for me to act strategically; I'm neither willing nor able to ignore the emotional strain these relationships put me under. I'm also unsure what position to adopt with my critics: Should I speak openly with them and let my disappointment show, or am I better off keeping my cards close to my chest? In his essay "Critique of Violence," Walter Benjamin asks whether conflicts can ever be resolved without violence. I myself believe that a certain amount of symbolic violence is unavoidable, and particularly within conflicts between friendly colleagues. It's crucial to strike the right balance—the less harm one inflicts upon the other, the better.

In any case, it is impossible to fully resolve such conflicts, if only because they lead to a reorganization of one's social group, during which former allies can turn into opponents. While my former friends and I would "like" each other's events on Facebook or Instagram, such gestures ceased with the publication of their criticisms of my book. With this, we symbolically signal to one another that we no longer support the other's activities, or even necessarily approve of them. Nor do we still invite each other to our conferences or events—which now take place online, if at all—as was once frequently the case. Viewed from the outside, it might appear as if we're currently doing all we can to avoid one another.

In my experience, there is just one method for rediscovering common ground in such situations: to speak some more. It is only when we sit across from someone that we develop a deeper understanding of their actions; we realize that, beyond the conflict, there is also much that connects us. But it is precisely such face-to-face communication that is currently hindered by the pandemic. Like many others, I've had my fill of walks in the cold by now, and my remaining energy for such excursions is reserved for my closest friends. On top of this, I've got enough to do just ensuring I mentally survive this endless lockdown. I need to conserve my energy, and so I can't afford to initiate potentially stressful and upsetting conversations with former friends. But as soon as lockdown is lifted and I have more energy—by which time I will hopefully also be vaccinated—I will attempt to organize meetings with them in cafés. Perhaps it will then be possible for us to reach a minimal consensus, despite our differences.

**1.20.2021**

My account of friendship seems to confirm Siegfried Kracauer's description of it, in his essay "On Friendship," as concealing a "conglomeration" of "thousands of events" within its "shell": "love, loyalty, courage, cowardice, hate, compassion, and pride." According to him, manifold processes and affects can be observed within these relationships that the notion of friendship is barely able to cover. Kracauer attempted to trace the specific features of friendship by comparing it to "acquaintanceship." I would describe some of my acquaintances as also being strongly "benefit-oriented," and so they might be considered a variety of utility friendship. And yet I have also cultivated acquaintances that yielded little in terms of usefulness. In Kracauer's view, relationships to acquaintances and colleagues (or "professional comrades," as he calls them) can be entirely "gratifying," and they often turn into friendships; from simple "shoptalk," he claims, there emerges a high degree of "intellectual familiarity" that is a source of happiness to those involved.

In my experience, the feelings of happiness Kracauer describes can also arise during conversations between acquaintances within the art world, such as when there is immediate agreement that a particular exhibition is problematic or the work of a certain artist promising. To quickly reach a consensus on a professional matter with acquaintances can be greatly satisfying. But while this agreement may feel like friendship, it is ultimately something different. Kracauer provides us with a criterion for distinguishing friendly relationships of this kind from true friendships: for as long as our relationships to our "professional comrades" are based on "professional consensus" and lack "deep personal sympathy," they are not friendships.

It was in fact the absence of this "deep human sympathy" that caused me to despair of some of my friends over time; our relationships were simply not as intimate or empathetic as they should have been—at least in my view. As already mentioned, Kracauer emphasizes the potential of acquaintanceships to bring happiness to those involved, provided they are based on a "brisk exchange of thoughts and ideas," on "shared enjoyment and convivial closeness," and on "freely coming and going and comfortable conversation." I have indeed enjoyed many pleasurable moments in the company of acquaintances; I have found our conversations to be inspiring, fulfilling, and enriching. But the influence of an acquaintance, Kracauer claims—and this is a fundamental difference to friends—does not go so far as to immediately contribute to our own sense of self; "their image does not live within us as an invisible companion on our journeys." Unlike our friends, then, our acquaintances are not admitted into our deeper consciousness, and they do not influence our inner development. And so, while they might stimulate us and bring us joy, they ultimately remain outside ourselves.

Unfortunately, Kracauer's definition of acquaintances and friends was exclusively limited to men, likely in part as a result of his time. He took the view that women only cultivated "emotional friendships"—purely affective bonds that he disparaged as lacking "intellectual sustenance." Kracauer's deprecation of friendships shaped by affect goes hand in hand with the sexist suggestion that women are "mindless" beings. (This way of thinking has not faded to this day. The fear of feelings—and their articulation—is often connected with a fierce aversion to everything "female," especially among some heterosexual men of my generation.) It's impossible to overlook Kracauer's misogyny and contempt for "emotional friendships" between women, even when viewing him as a product of his time.

But there are other aspects of his reflections on friendship that are useful in considering contemporary relationships, such as his thoughts on friendship versus love. The question of how much friendship sexual partnerships can endure before it poses a danger has been discussed in self-help books (and women's magazines) for decades. In Kracauer's view, sexual love and friendship have one thing in common: they each capture "the entire soul of a person." This observation seems fitting to me, since both my closest friends and my life partner touch me deeply, penetrating my most inner being. But while Kracauer (like Socrates and Montaigne before him) emphatically characterizes friendship as a "permeation of souls," he also notes that it does not lead to the "melding of existence" to which love aspires. While a friendship brings two people together in harmony, love aims to fuse their "entire lives." And so it is: I don't necessarily want to share my everyday life with my friends; I'd rather choose when to meet them. My desire to form a household with friends was never that strong—I associate such situations with disputes over shopping or cleaning schedules, which would put a strain on those friendships. In my romantic relationships, too, only rarely and with some reluctance have I committed to the project of "cohabitation." I cling to the autonomy that my own apartment provides. That I have not only the much-invoked room of my own but a whole apartment does not, however, mean I am unwilling to involve myself in my partner's living conditions or that our relationship lacks commitment; on the contrary, it's precisely because we meet each other as autonomous individuals that I can devote myself to him with my body and soul.

According to Kracauer, there is no love that is not also "accompanied" by friendship, and no true friendship can get by without love. My love for my partner would be indeed a flawed one if it lacked a dimension of friendship, while conversely, what I feel for my friends is undoubtedly also love—if mostly platonic. The "mostly" here makes it clear how permeable these concepts are, and it's true that some of my friendships also have a sexual undertone. Moreover, most of my romantic relationships began as friendships, with the passion coming only after we had thoroughly gotten to know one another. Friendship often feeds into love, then, and yet I resist the notion that I am my partner's best friend. I am not attracted to the idea of taking on two roles—that of the friend and that of the lover—and I prefer him to seek his friends elsewhere. For if I were his best friend, this would endanger our relationship as lovers. While our romantic relationship should display elements of friendship, it's ultimately coded as something different—as love, that is.

**2.17.2021**

My teenage daughter Calliope informed me over dinner yesterday that I—unlike her friends—have not been a "significant person" for her in recent years; instead, my role in her life has been that of mother and caregiver. I was initially shocked that she would deny me this function—after all, in sociological terms, a significant person is someone with whom one has a close personal relationship, and toward whom one orients oneself. And I'm apparently not this person to my own daughter? I now wonder if my assumption that we have maintained a deep connection since her birth might have been wishful thinking on my part; my influence over her is clearly not nearly as great as I thought. In recent years especially, other figures in her life have become more important role models for her, such as her friends. I am tortured by the thought that being constantly busy means I didn't catch that she has increasingly closed herself off to me, and that she now keeps much to herself. Her comment cut me to the quick.

Following our conversation, and after taking several deep breaths, I reminded myself that Calliope is going through puberty and must do all she can to distance herself from me. To claim that I am not a significant person in her life is certainly an effective means of creating this distance. She also knows my trigger points better than others—she's well aware that she can get to me and make me feel guilty with such a comment.

Her statement was aimed at giving me the impression that I, as her mother, am of little importance to her—and this was meant to widen the gulf between us.

I lay awake in bed for a long time after our conversation, pondering the meaning of what she said. I managed to come up with a more positive interpretation: perhaps Calliope simply wanted to let me know that she had never seen me as a "friend" (i.e. significant person), since I have never stepped out of the role of mother in our relationship. Her statement could even have been a veiled compliment; perhaps she was actually praising me for the fact I have never tried to be her best friend. After all, many mothers (and celebrity mothers in lifestyle magazines especially) boast that they are their daughter's "best girlfriend." Conversely, I have also known daughters who enthusiastically describe their mothers as the most trusted and significant people in their lives: the mother as best friend. In this context, I am particularly troubled by the term "mini-me," as some mothers like to refer to their daughters. Any claim to difference seems to be denied to the mini-me from the outset, with the daughter downgraded to a copy and defined entirely in terms of an origin that is understood biologically.

My wish for my daughter, by contrast, is that she establish herself in a milieu whose initiation rituals (especially for young women) are less severe than those of my own. If I see her beginning to go down a route similar to mine, I secretly hope she will later change her mind. By contrast, I would be happy if she succeeded in developing those facets of her personality that are alien to me—like inner peace or a talent for the natural sciences—and which I therefore admire all the more. I mistrust the dynastic principle that prevails within the art establishment and hope Calliope will free herself from familial models instead of reproducing them. All too often, I have observed the children of renowned critics or gallerists either taking the same path as their parents or benefiting enormously from a parent's reputation in their own artistic careers. The fact that they usually carry a recognizable name puts them at an advantage from the get-go: they already belong to the art world and so are automatically awarded a certain degree of trust, with no need to further prove themselves. Those who do not enjoy the privilege of such familial capital spend years relegated to the margins before being granted admittance. Since I myself chose a profession far removed from those of my parents (economic adviser and physiotherapist), it's hard for me to muster respect for the beneficiaries of nepotism, whose cards are stacked so favorably from the start. At the same time, I am aware that my relationship with my daughter is far more attentive and trusting and less ambivalent than was the case with me and my parents. Calliope need not demonstrate her rejection of me by choosing an entirely different direction in her career. If she is interested in painting and writing, then this is ultimately a great compliment to me (and to her artistic father, my ex-husband). It therefore goes without saying that we support her in all her activities.

That aside, I do want to ensure I live up to my role of mother and the responsibilities it entails, instead of seeking Calliope's friendship. After all, it wasn't easy for me to adjust to this role, since my view of my own mother meant that for a long time I associated this position with victimhood and sacrifice. The prospect of becoming a mother myself filled me with terror; it took years of therapy before I trusted myself to develop a different way of thinking about and practicing motherhood. Being a mother did not come easily to me; I worked hard for it, and I have no interest in swapping this role for that of a friend. When I give my daughter advice, sympathize with her, or feel happy for her, then I do so from the position of her mother, not her mother-friend.

I imagine we will be able to have a more friend-like relationship once I am no longer responsible for her—that is, once she is of legal age. In my view, mothers who continue to treat their fifty-year-old sons and daughters as children are every bit as problematic as those who treat their teenage daughters like friends—they seem unable to adapt to their new roles as the mothers of independent adults. As for Calliope and me, our relationship is some way away from being a friendship. If she uses slang with me or curses, I remind her that I am not one of her friends. I do my best to ensure the claims of the mother are staked out clearly in our relationship.

My love pact with Calliope is naturally of a different nature to those made between friends (and to those that lovers will one day make with her). My love for my daughter is unconditional, while friendships and love affairs can, by contrast, always be terminated. It is this unconditionality of my love for Calliope that allows her to hurl any insult or attack at me she likes; she knows she will never lose me, despite her hurtful words. And yet I must resist when she pushes the limits. It was for this reason that I let her know this morning that her description of me as an "insignificant person" had offended me. She noted this without any visible emotion, before returning to her FaceTime call with her best friend.

**2.19.2021**

Calliope managed to talk me into getting a small dog. We picked him up from the animal shelter yesterday; he's a Bolognese who can easily be taken along on journeys since he fits in a large handbag. Calliope won me over with the argument that she, as an only child, needs a dog as a companion in this endless pandemic. While I find the idea of keeping a dog in the city to be problematic, the benefits of a having pet are obvious to me in this case, since it promises to relieve her loneliness. Since the first lockdown in March 2020, Calliope has spent most of her free time alone in her room, where she either listens to her online lessons or communicates with her friends digitally. The dog means she is now forced to leave the house several times a day. While I have barely been able to get her to go for a walk during lockdown, she now enthusiastically takes to the streets with him. We named him Apollo after the ancient god—a sort of higher being tasked with making us happy. I must admit, he is adorable. Calliope is doing an exemplary job of taking care of him, and I practically have to beg her to allow me to take him out. We took our first walk together today. While cleaning up his excrement with plastic gloves will take some getting used to, owning a dog means constantly meeting new people and falling into conversation with them. One has a shared object to bond over.

Today, my borrowed companion and I ran into someone whom I have known for a long time. Turning into the tranquil Gipsstraße with Apollo, I suddenly saw Paula, standing alongside her own dog. We had not seen or spoken to one another since she put an end to our friendship many months ago, even though we are both regulars at the same bars and restaurants. It was similar to my chance encounter with Peter at the Hamburger Bahnhof, with the exception that, this time, our dogs also approached each other. We struck up a conversation, returning to our familiar routine as if there had been no rift between us at all. We discussed the pandemic and its impact on the cultural sector, reported on the current state of our work projects, and each informed the other of how we were keeping fit during lockdown: she with online kickboxing sessions, I with online barre sessions.

At some point, I gathered the courage to ask her why she had broken off contact with me. Was she really so appalled by my decision to curate a commercial exhibition that she no longer wanted anything to do with me? Or was there actually another reason she had distanced herself? Paula visibly squirmed in response to my questions; it was clearly uncomfortable for her to broach the subject of our split. Her voice barely audible, she muttered that she'd been having a rough time back then and had wanted to burn bridges with all her acquaintances. Her retreat had nothing to do with me and my projects. What had offended her was the fact that I had refused to lend her money, despite her highly precarious situation. I attempted to explain my viewpoint at the time—that it would only have put a further strain on our friendship for her to be in my debt. She didn't seem convinced by this argument. Nonetheless, her tone became more conciliatory, and she said how happy she would be if we could reestablish our friendship and have more interaction in the future. I told her I would also like this.

I was surprised by my own words. Hadn't I sworn that I would never resume friendly contact with her? Hadn't her decision to be done with me for reasons I couldn't comprehend represented a breach of trust? Now, in conversation, I found her so likeable and familiar that our quarrel simply evaporated; it seemed to lie far in the past, as if overwritten by our current understanding for one another—we simply have too much in common to let a rift drive us apart. The sense of harmony that arose between us on the street meant I was unable to bear a grudge against her. Beyond this, Paula also seemed to have changed. While she used to remind me of my old self in the 1980s, when I pitilessly judged other people, she now seemed more understanding when talking about others. She, too, has apparently moved on from this practice of personal evaluation, in which the possible verdicts were limited to thumbs up or thumbs down; no gray areas, no ambivalences. We would often slip into this arrogant pose in our younger lives, criticizing others for their taste while ignoring the fallibility of our own judgment. At that time, the defining criterion for someone meeting our standards was their sense of style or coolness. Paula could be merciless in this respect, with people she had once seen as hip deemed to be no longer so just a short time later. She discarded them with a verve and brutality that now seems questionable to me. I am still interested in the language and laws of fashion, but I no longer want to diss someone just because their taste doesn't seem up to date.

Paula didn't speak badly of others during our encounter or comment on their current looks. It seemed as if staying at the forefront of fashion with her outfits had become as unimportant to her as it now is to me—she was wearing the same pieces she'd had on during our last encounter two years ago. It's likely that criteria such as friendliness, attentiveness, and empathy have also become more important to her in the time since—both in herself and in others. (In my experience, hipsters can rarely be relied on in emotional terms.) We once encouraged each other to badmouth or gossip about others, but this form of hate speech is no longer an option. It smacks not only of a lack of understanding of the differences that exist among people, but also of a high degree of self-righteousness and aggression. Self-hatred is projected outward in the form of malice directed at others.

Immediately after our chance meeting, Paula sent me

a series of text messages in which she expressed her joy that we had resumed contact. I now ask myself whether her newly professed interest in a friendly relationship with me might indeed be instrumentally driven, and I ask myself why I am asking myself this. Could her approaching me now be because my star seems to be burning a little more brightly again? In spite of the negative reviews of my book, the situation is different to when we split back in 2018—the year of my seeming success, which in reality, as I've already mentioned, was overshadowed by multiple challenges. In comparison to 2018, I'm now more firmly in the saddle—I just published a short text that was well received, and I curated another group show in a gallery, which got positive reviews. So it might be no coincidence that it's at this very moment that Paula is attempting to get closer to me.

I catch myself speculating that she does perhaps want something from me—money, or other forms of support. Repudiating my mistrustful self, I resolve to remain in friendly contact with her. But I also tell myself that I do not want to allow our relationship to become too intimate. It won't be easy to maintain this balance, since a part of me tends to be overly open with others; during our reunion with the dogs, there was actually no need for me to immediately tell Paula of my problems with those friends who were hard on my book in their reviews, for example. Perhaps in the future I'll think more carefully about whom I trust and with what. Then again, maybe not.

**2.20.2021**

I have now made you, the reader of these pages, an involuntary accomplice in my strategic considerations. And yet by subjecting the text to my stylistic and compositional ideals, I also attempt to place my secrets at a distance. Confidential information is presented in a literary form that fulfills my duty of discretion. My interest here is not in revealing my true or authentic self. In writing these notes in diaristic form, my aim is instead to demonstrate the embeddedness of this "I" within social relationships and friendship networks.

When it comes to the diary as literary form, one of my key influences (in addition to Marie Luise Kaschnitz) is Max Frisch. On the one hand, Frisch had the unspeakable habit—as can be observed in *Montauk*—of treating the women in his life as fundamentally other, as exotic creatures that he lustfully ogled but never respected. As an author of diaries as well as diaristic and autofictional novels, on the other hand, he accomplished a great deal: from Frisch onward, the diary has been considered a literary form equal to that of the novel, and one that is itself capable of taking on novelistic qualities. His diaries do not merely record his spontaneous impressions and experiences, they also serve as a platform for reflections on his time, and as a testing ground for experiments in different literary approaches. Frisch repeatedly reworked the language of his diaries, meaning they do not display the notelike character that is otherwise typical of the genre. The literary role models he refers to are (unfortunately) all men—above all Peter Handke, whose book *A Sorrow Beyond Dreams* he greatly admired. Frisch writes in *Montauk* that Handke's book about his dead mother gave him the license to say "I" in his novels; this right may now be claimed by all other authors (including myself) with relatively little risk.

While I, too, hold Handke's book on mourning in high regard, my primary influence comes from those contemporary authors who have been labeled with the term "autofiction," such as Annie Ernaux, Violaine Huisman, Rachel Cusk, and Deborah Levy. They gave me the courage to allow an I to speak in my own texts—one that proves to be entirely social. The power of social attributions is manifested in this I; it is permeated by external circum-stances such as those of friendship.

Autofictional writing runs the risk of indiscretion, as Frisch himself grappled with in his diaries. In addition to his preoccupation with this danger, he also expresses his regret in *Selections from the Berlin Diary* that by not writing down his experiences, he had "buried them in his continued life," a life he somewhat maudlinly describes as having remained "concealed" in his previous books. At the start of the 1970s, it seemed to Frisch as if his whole life had passed him by in his writing. It was as if his books had "missed" his life—a shortcoming he clearly wanted to make up for with *Montauk*.

While I find Frisch's pathos disconcerting, I can relate to his feeling that something vital escaped him in his writing. I, too, had the impression in recent years that my art-historical texts lack those other things that equally matter to me in my life, and so the desire grew in me to find a new way of writing that would allow me to record everything else that moves me. Frisch also describes the drawbacks of his resolution to disclose everything from that point on; writing his *Berlin Diary*, he reports, he was filled with shame at the thought of its future readers. Above all, he wanted to show consideration toward his wife—a consideration that, at the same time, he considered to be "treacherous," since it ultimately served merely as "self-protection." I do not agree that consideration is ultimately a means of protecting ourselves against the outrage of others. For consideration is fundamentally related to others: we do not want their feelings to be hurt by finding themselves mentioned in the pages of a book. Because taking account of other people's feelings requires us to imagine and empathize with their emotional states, and this has little do with self-protection. I also wonder what it is that bothers Frisch so much about self-protection—does he reject the impulse to protect himself since he associates this prudence with cowardice and a lack of (manly) heroism? For me, self-protection is something to be valued. It's important to ensure one doesn't throw oneself to the wild animals unprotected, as my therapist always says. In other words, it's important to carefully consider in which situations and to whom one shows vulnerability and exposes oneself.

That Frisch primarily associates consideration with self-protection makes sense when reading *Montauk*. His life partners are not spared in the book; both Ingeborg Bachmann—with whom he had a liaison, and who was already deceased at the time he wrote the book—and his then wife Marianne are mentioned by name. That Frisch detailed his affair with a young American while still married must have been painful for Marianne. That he knew and accepted the pain it would cause her is also signaled by a literary trick on his part: *Montauk* contains a message to the author, likely written by Marianne herself. In it, she informs him that she has not lived with him as "literary material," and that she therefore forbids him from writing about her. Frisch then incorporates this ban into his book, thus formulating a performative objection to her demand. With this, he demonstrates to Marianne and the rest of the world that he, as a writer, ultimately has the upper hand; even her refusal to function as material is exploited by him for literary purposes. Viewed in methodological terms, however, Frisch's process was consistent. He wanted to present the true circumstances of his life; "the truth is bearable to man," as an advertising slogan quoted at one point in the book puts it. For the sake of truth, then, literature must be inconsiderate. Marianne's request not to be used as material thus had to be fed into the narrative as material.

The situation is a different one in my case: I make an effort to ensure I do not hurt or embarrass anyone with this book. Nor do I want to breach anyone's "personality rights." While my protagonists have something in common with the actual people in my life, they are invented figures; no one appears by their real name, and each of my figures is composed of multiple real people. So while Frisch found himself confronted by his wife's request not to write about her, I experienced the opposite: yesterday, my friend Carla implored me to include her in the book in a form recognizable to all. She is keen to play a role within it and to appear alongside my other friends on an equal footing. Perhaps she hopes that the success of this book—however unlikely it may be—might rub off on her. In any case, she seems confident that my description of her and our friendship will turn out to be a positive one. Why else would she insist that I grant her a proper place in my book on true and useful friendships? I've decided to do her this favor; the following entry will include an appearance by Carla.

**3.10.2021**

A few weeks ago, I accompanied Calliope to school to help her clean out her locker, since the students have been asked to store their things at home during remote learning. This transfer of educational materials to the domestic environment seems to symbolize the fact that the responsibility for schooling now falls to parents more than ever. So as I stood before Calliope's locker, stuffed with papers, pens, and sporting equipment, I felt depressed at the thought that the formally public task of education had now been shifted to the private sphere.

Close by, I spotted a woman helping her daughter clear out her own things. It was early morning, and I could see from the pale features visible above her mask that she was as tired as I was. Another glance revealed that she was wearing the same oversize black fake-fur jacket as me, from the current Acne collection. We stood across from one another as lookalikes. And yet instead of feeling as if our singular sense of style was threatened by this reproduction of our look by another, we attempted to communicate friendly smiles using our eyes. We did not react with horror, as the lifestyle press reports of celebrities on the red carpet who have spotted someone else wearing the same dress as them; there was no sign of "mimetic rivalry." According to the anthropologist René Girard, this occurs whenever the same thing is desired (or imitated) by another. With us, though, no trace of envy or jealousy. Instead, the sense of mutual sympathy was based—as it so often is at the beginning of a friendship—on a presumption of similarity. By approaching each other, we signaled how happy we were to meet someone who shared our fashion sense in such an unexpected setting.

We introduced ourselves: her name is Madelaine, she is an actress, has two daughters, and is married to a camera operator. We spoke about our private and professional circumstances while running through our favorite designers and fashion preferences. We clarified where we had each purchased the Acne jacket—the item that connected us. Not only did our tastes immediately "click," but we also seemed a good fit in emotional terms. I was particularly taken by Madelaine's warmhearted nature. Her loud manner of speaking, accompanied by elaborate gestures, indicates a penchant for the dramatic—another thing we have in common. A meeting of two drama queens.

We swapped phone numbers, resolving to go shopping together once the lockdown was over. Since then, we have been sending each other photos of clothes we find in sales on our favorite websites; as soon as we start eyeing a new piece, we ask the other for her opinion on it. Yesterday Madelaine went to the department store KaDeWe. She bombarded me with selfies of her in a changing cubicle, trying on various sweaters and pairs of trousers. If I thought an item suited her and the price was right, I texted her my approval.

What is developing between us is not just a fashion friendship but something both broader and deeper, since we are on a similar emotional wavelength. Within just a few days, not only has Madelaine risen to the position of my personal fashion advisor, but she has also become a trusted confidant in my parenting and relationship problems—while I, in turn, play the same role for her. We found each other; this, at least, was how another "school mother" who witnessed our initial meeting in front of the lockers put it. Our shared outlook on fashion means we have forged a close bond, but one that largely excludes others—those, that is, who don't have the financial means and also do not share our knowledge of or interest in the subject.

Fashion, then, is the domain where our mutual understanding (based on a certain degree of privilege) first revealed itself. Our harmonious relationship means I don't mind if she "copies" me by purchasing a coat I already own; on the contrary, her decision to buy it reinforces my sense of my own taste—and with this, by extension, of my personality, since my self is also expressed within these aesthetic judgments. By wearing the same coat, we also make the depth of our connection known to others. When we took a walk together yesterday in matching outfits, for example, we appeared as two friends showing off their bond to the world. Our agreement on matters of fashion accelerates and deepens our friendship.

Carla, too, was initially a fashion friend of mine. Like me, Carla has been anchored in the art world for many years, first as an artist and now also as a successful gallerist. Our behavior might be cited as proof of Georg Simmel's thesis that the pursuit of sameness and the desire to be different go hand in hand in fashion. For instance, I often wear what Carla wears—that is, our clothes give us a similar appearance. We find a connection by wearing the same outfits. And yet by orienting ourselves toward each other and orchestrating shared looks, we also "fashion" ourselves as singular individuals; we are similar and yet different.

That fashion targets our capacity for imitation, our mimetic desire, is something I have often experienced with Carla. I remember once sitting with her in a café at the height of summer. I was wearing an airy shoulderless dress by Isabel Marant, and Carla was so impressed by it that she immediately ordered one on her phone. When we go shopping together, we often leave the boutique looking like Hannie and Annie—identically dressed friends happy that what looks good on one also suits the other. We gladly inform one another about bargains or new fashion discoveries, without keeping such privileged information for ourselves. When it comes to fashion, the results of our research are always shared.

But where my nascent friendship with Madelaine lacks any instrumental dimension, my relationship with Carla is occasionally characterized by its usefulness. We have often been on vacation together, and these trips were generally harmonious, except when she would try to rope me into helping her with her work. I recall one such instance when I had asked her to leave the art world at home; despite this, she asked after breakfast one day if I would proofread a press release for her. She was so persistent that I eventually gave in. But the fact that she had managed to avail herself of my labor even when I was on holiday made me slightly resentful. Carla sees things differently though—she is convinced that it is only natural to work for your friend. For her, this type of labor is a gesture of helpfulness that is intrinsic to friendship. But I wonder about the border between "helping" and "using" one another. Is me working for her a natural, helpful gesture, or does she exploit my labor when asking me to write her press release? It would be wrong for me to fault her personally; instead, her behavior should be seen as a reflection of the instrumental nature of art-world friendships.

To some extent, this smooth transition between "help" and "exploitation" represents a déformation professionelle of the art world. Sounding out others for the benefits they might offer is a widespread survival strategy within this habitat. I, too, am equally influenced by such considerations, and I have trouble freeing myself from them even when on vacation. Here, I recall a yoga retreat where I met a collector to whom I later offered a subscription to my journal and edition series. Since the boundary between leisure time and professional life is fluid within the art world, it would be too much to expect Carla to abstain from business entirely during her vacation. One learns early on in the art business that every opportunity that presents itself must be capitalized upon, every encounter profited from. And these considerations also repeatedly play a role in how one behaves among friends—just as they permeate vacations spent together.

While I do not compete with Carla or Madelaine on the level of fashion, this does not mean I am always comfortable with other women copying my taste in clothing. A few years ago, I gave a rich collector whom I had "befriended" a tour of Berlin's boutiques. A short time previously, I had asked for a leather jacket that I could not (yet) afford to be put aside for me in one such store; I planned to save for it, and I hoped that the owner of the boutique would reserve it for me in the meantime. Following our visit, I learned from the store owner that the collector had purchased it for herself just a short time later, after I had pointed it out to her—that is, she had snatched it away from me. This example demonstrates the aggressive power of "mimetic rivalry" in its purest form: it was through my own desire that the desire of the collector was triggered. She wanted to have the same piece I had my heart set on, no matter what. By making her purchase, she also demonstrated the power of money; in the fashion world, the people given priority are those that can pay. The fact that I was so set on having this jacket made it irresistible to her. And yet she could have had any other jacket she wanted. By claiming "my" leather jacket above all others, and by imitating my desire, she ensured I was eliminated as a rival. For this magnificent specimen of a jacket was the last of its kind.

**3.20.2021**

In making these observations, I run the risk of being branded superficial and consumerist. While it may be acceptable for me to view fashion as a practice that contributes to identity, to spend most of my money on fashion items, and hours prowling various websites and boutiques informing myself about their new collections, seems frivolous. Wouldn't it be better for me to invest my money in something more long-lasting, and aren't there better ways of spending my time than researching fashion for hours on end? Some readers will also wonder how someone can simultaneously be both a fashion victim and an intellectual, and what deficit I'm compensating for with the items I obsess over.

I see no contradiction here, however. For I reflect upon my "addiction" just as much as I occasionally succumb to it. And in my view, the language of fashion can best be understood by those who speak it themselves. While I'm not entirely transparent with myself regarding my enthusiasm for fashion, I am aware it might be rooted in deep-seated insecurity and anxiety. Within the milieu of the art world, especially, I feel better equipped to face social situations when I have something new on. To wear a dress by a hip designer whom I also admire to an opening is like carrying a shield that makes me appear more confident in the eyes of others and less vulnerable in my own. My mood lifted by the new outfit, I'm able to float into the exhibition space; it stills my fear of the judgmental gaze of others and gives me the (imagined) sense of security that no one, now, can touch me. While the notion that fashion places me "at the forefront" and simultaneously serves as a sort of armor is a phantasmatic illusion, this does not make it any less effective. By dressing fashionably, I show that I am capable of adapting to the changeable; I let it be known that I am informed and agile, but also someone who yields to fashion's norms. Fashion is therefore a cultural authority that bolsters and strengthens me—the designer dress lends extra emphasis to me and my concerns. And it's not only at gallery openings that I strive for a fashionably informed look, but also when meeting with friends. This helps me to present an image of myself that I can feel reasonably satisfied with. Fashion carries me beyond myself, and dedicating myself to it can be uplifting.

Throughout my life, I have always given preference to the staged over the (supposedly) authentic. The reasons for this are both philosophical and biographical. In philosophical terms, I do not believe in an authenticity beyond the staged; on closer inspection, all phenomena fall somewhere between the poles of authentic and staged. In addition, I have been encouraged to enact certain roles since childhood, and with highly positive results. My father, especially, particularly valued me when I "looked good," was well dressed, and put on a convincing performance. Deep down, I likely still believe I will only be loved if I stage my "self" as skillfully and stylishly as possible.

What was once a sad necessity in the battle for the love and attention of my father has, by now, transformed into a highly enjoyable part of my everyday life. The psychological pressure is less pronounced than it once was, since I now have people close to me who couldn't care less what I wear, who value me regardless and barely register if I have something new on. It's for this reason, too, that my former mania for self-staging has eased up somewhat—I've learned that low-key looks can function just as well as spectacular ones. Nonetheless, it is downright exhilarating to wear a new top, and to show it off to my fashion friends. I therefore have no intention of abandoning my passion yet.

**3.23.2021**

Among those friends who do share my enthusiasm for fashion, there is one—her name is Leontine, and she is a filmmaker—whom I generally only speak with over the phone; one might describe our relationship as a phone friendship. We call each other several times a week, talking for hours at a time and discussing everything: our favorite fashion designers, feuilleton articles, novels that have inspired us, exhibitions we enjoyed, films on Netflix worth watching, and notable incidents within our circle of friends. Cultural criticism, gossip, textual analysis, and small talk all flow into one another in these conversations, and we are mostly united in our interpretations of the cultural products and events we discuss. And this even though we each arrive at our conclusions via different paths: she impulsively and intuitively, and I with a view to the historical circumstances within which a cultural product is embedded and which make it seem relevant or questionable.

Only seldomly do we meet in person; speaking over the phone seems to suit us better. It only confronts us with a fragment of the other—with a voice, that is, in which the body of the speaker nonetheless resonates. On the rare occasion that we do meet in a café, the physical presence of the other can be overwhelming. We only feel close to one another on the condition that we do not actually get physically close.

Kracauer offered apposite reflections on friendships of this kind, which, according to him, are beneficial since immediate coexistence between those of the "same nature" often leads to "friction." To put up with a friend "in real life," then, is far from easy, and so it's tempting to reach for the phone instead, as a way of maintaining distance. According to Kracauer, this distance can even intensify the feeling of friendship; for him, the presence of the other is not an "absolute requirement" for such a bond. For what friendships involve is something fundamentally different: two individuals who find and grow on each other. At the same time, Kracauer argues, alienation must also be permitted within a friendship to some degree. The relationship must be elastic enough to allow for the possibility that the other will become unfamiliar.

The same is true of Leontine and me, since the sense of familiarity we feel when speaking on the phone—this form of finding each other—cannot readily be kept alive in our real-life encounters. Sitting across from one another in a café, it's as if we were meeting for the first time; the friction and estrangement Kracauer speaks of is sensed by us both. That we permit this unfamiliarity instead of seeing it as a danger to our friendship, is, to me, the great potential of our bond. Although its significance is, naturally, limited by the fact that we can only tolerate the voice of the other—while their bodily presence, by contrast, is something we still need to get used to. This partial acceptance speaks to the difficulty of fully embracing the other within a friendship. I myself think such complete acceptance is difficult to realize in practice; we always block out a part of the friend's character in order to remain friends with them.

**4.1.2021**

To grasp a person in all their complexity, then, is impossible; even my close friends Solange and Majorie are alien to me in some respects. And vice versa: while I want to expose my inner life to my friends, I don't give everything away. Only a fraction of what goes through my head forces its way outside, and I hold a lot back for myself. I don't want to hurt my friends, and there are certain thoughts I also don't reveal out of shame. If I told them everything, I would run the risk of appearing unlovable in their eyes. I am often a bit too judgmental, and I tend to be too merciless in my analysis of certain events. It is also rare for me to speak of the less than flattering psychological profiles I create of others. I thus censor my inner monologues before bothering Solange and Majorie with them.

The remnants of what I hold back—the things that might make me appear less sympathetic—are recorded in my diaries. And so while it might sound pathetic, my journal is my best friend. In keeping a diary, I address a "fictional I," as Elias Canetti called it in his essay "Dialogue with a Violent Partner" (the "violent partner" being his diary). The diary "I" whom I speak to in its pages displays numerous similarities with my other I without being identical to it; it is me and then again not. This "fictional I" has the crucial advantage, Canetti claims, of genuinely listening and never turning away. It is always there.

One might indeed impose anything on a diary. It is precisely because its patience knows no limits that the things one experiences may be intensified beyond all measure in its pages. My diary therefore tends toward the excessive in its description of events. Canetti notes of this phenomenon that man "actually consists of exaggeration," but that this "faculty" need not be fought against—and certainly not as a writer, I would

Isabelle Graw is the publisher of the journal *Texte zur Kunst*, which she cofounded with Stefan Germer (1958–98) in 1990, and professor of art history and art theory at the Hochschule für Bildende Künste – Städelschule, Frankfurt am Main. Her previous books include *Three Cases of Value Reflection: Ponge, Whitten, Banksy* (2021), *In Another World: Notes,2014–2017* (2020), *The Love of Painting: Genealogy of a Success Medium* (2018), and *High Price: Art Between the Market and Celebrity Culture* (2010).
She lives in Berlin.

Isabelle Graw
On the Benefits of Friendship

Published by Sternberg Press

Translated from the German by Ben Caton

Editor: Max Bach
Proofreading: Michela Parkin
Design: Studio Markus Weisbeck
Printing: Tallinn Book Printers, Estonia

Cover: Sturtevant, *Warhol Flowers*, 1970.
Synthetic polymer silk screen on canvas,
56 × 56 × 2 cm. © Estate Sturtevant, Paris.
Photo: Charles Duprat.
Courtesy of Thaddaeus Ropac gallery
London/Paris/Salzburg/Seoul.

ISBN 978-3-95679-652-4



First published 2023, reprinted 2024

Distributed by The MIT Press, Art Data, Les presses du réel, and Idea Books

Sternberg Press
71–75 Shelton Street
UK-London WC2H 9JQ
www.sternberg-press.com